Industrial Security Management

Industrial Security Management

Editor

R K Sinha

Vitasta
Let Knowledge Spread

Published by
Vitasta Publishing Pvt. Ltd.
2/15, Ansari Road, Daryaganj,
New Delhi - 110 002
info@vitastapublishing.com

ISBN: 978-93-80828-58-9

First Edition 2012
3rd Reprint 2022
MRP ₹650

Layout and Cover Design by Vitasta Publishing Pvt. Ltd.
Printed by Vits Press, New Delhi

Acknowledgement

I acknowledge the valuable contribution of Ms Jyoti Sinha, Mr Praveen Kumar and Ms Seema Sharma in collecting suitable articles for this book from amongst various papers presented in IISSM annual seminars, workshops and various short term training courses in past 20 years.

Thanks is also due to Ms Ratna Sinha, joint secretary, IISSM for monitoring and administrating this project, on a day-to-day basis. I also acknowledge support of Lt Gen (Retd) Prem Sagar, director general, IISSM and Brig (Retd) S Sreeramulu, deputy director general (Academic Services), IISSM, without whose cooperation completion of this project in record time was not possible.

Ravindra Sinha

Editor & Executive Chairman, IISSM

Content

Foreword

After Industrial revolution, in late 18th Century/early 19th century, growth of industries in India also started taking place. Jamsetji Nusserwanji Tata established TATA Iron & Steel Company (TISCO) in Jamshedpur in the year 1907. Even before that several Textiles Mills in Mumbai and Jute mills in Kolkata had started. Industrial development started taking place in various parts of India in the core sectors like Jute, Steel, Sugar, Cement, Textile, and Paper and later on in Fertilizers and Chemicals. Sahu Shati Prasad Jain established an integrated industrial city–"Dalmianagar" near Dehri-on-sone in Bihar and Seth Gujar Mal Modi established another industrial township named as "Modi Nagar" in the district Ghaziabad of Uttar Pradesh. Both these industrial township had plants of cement, sugar, paper, engineering, vegetable oil etc. Initially, engineering industry was confined to the activities connected mainly to the Indian Railway and Sugar Industry only. Bharat Wagon, Burn Standard etc. were the main players in engineering industry to begin with. After independence, Hindustan Motors of Birla Group and Tata Engineering and Locomotives Works came as pioneers in automobile industry. On the request of the then Prime Minister, Shri Jawahar Lal Nehru, Bharat Ratna J R D Tata also started "Lakme" to fill the vacuum in the cosmetic industry to meet requirement of woman India. A number of Jute mills had started in West Bengal and hundreds of textile mills had started in and around the city of Mumbai. Hundreds of sugar mills came up into existence in the Sugar-cane producing states of Maharashtra, Karnataka, Tamilnadu, Uttar Predesh and Bihar. All these initial industries had a typical set-up. They all had strong and high parameter walls, a gate office, a factory or plant area, an office or administrative building, an officers' colony, which also had a guest house and a worker's colony an electrical sub-station etc. Some industries, where mining was a part of activity, there was a mines area, an explosive magazine for storage for explosives and in most of the cases a railway siding. Therefore, industrial security till late 70s only meant high walls and strong gates. Security was considered chowkidari or in most of the cases "watch and ward". It was considered that if the parameter wall is high and inescapable and gates are strong enough, a few chowkidars can prevent all losses. This was somewhat true also during that time because, the losses were mainly from external thefts. Employees were loyal and used to work generation after generation for the same owners. Till late 80's or even till mid 90's Security Services was considered as a "necessary evil" by the management. Security is a job, in fact, that the more effectively it works, the more useless it appears.

Now, the scenario has completely changed. External thieves in search of steel scrapes, pumps, motors and copper wires have found wagon breaking and road robberies more profitable and less risky preposition and industrial thieves have diverted and diversified their business. But internal thefts have significantly increased. Thefts of valuables, finish products, valuable information and data, CDs, floppies, pen drives are causing greater losses to the industry. 20 years back physical security thefts used to contribute almost 70% of the losses and internal thefts. Frauds, misappropriation and embezzlement contributed the balance. Now, situation has reversed. Almost 70 to 80% thefts are internal and mostly contribute to economic offences and unethical practices. I will narrate a classic example. About 15 years back CEO of a large Chemical Industry called me to seek my assistance for an investigation. The company had a turnover in thousands of crores. The main activity of the company was producing a proprietary basic chemical which was mostly being used for producing a particular end product which was a fast moving item in construction projects. What had happened was that one day the end producer company ownership decided to do backward integration of the product. The argument was that our almost 100% raw material is this particular chemical and we have to depend on one basic chemical producer for this. Why do not we go in for manufacturing? Argument was okay but, from where to get the technologies? The technology was the proprietary item of the factory producing that chemical. Then they resorted to unethical practices. They offer a salary to the factory manager of the basic chemical producer which he could not refuse. And, thus the biggest technology theft in India took place. The 80% produce of the basic chemical produce was being consumed by the end- product producer. Then what was the option left for the basic chemical producer? To shut down the factory or to do the forward integration of the factory and start producing the end product itself. They went for the second option and that costs them a fortune! A new factory, new set of employees, sales force, branding, huge advertisement companies and so on. This was the cost of not watching the activities of a "Key employee"! Therefore, security scenario has changed and present day security managers have to develop their expertise in evolving innovative, counter measures to address latest sources of losses and prevent latest methodology of criminal activities. They also have to learn how to mitigate various kinds of possible risks arising out of fire and accidents and disasters. The present book talks about multiple dimensions of Industrial Security with different perspectives and addresses almost all issues which I have mentioned above.

Chapter 1 emphasizes that security and safety aspects should become part and parcel of all training programs and each and everyone who is working in the industry should be aware of industrial security. Thus, training of security and fire risks to the non-security personnel is more important.

Chapter 2 explains aspect of motivation of the security personnel and various influences like attitude of the group, selection and placement, training, supervision, special emphasis program and media which can affect individual motivation.

Chapter 3 focuses on role of Intelligence in Industrial Security. Intelligence provides knowledge of the forces endangering or likely to end safety and without this knowledge no security system can function. Various types of intelligence like criminal, labour, counter, intelligence for executive protection and vigilance should be looked into by industrial units depending upon its threat perception and vulnerability.

Chapter 4 delves into latest equipments for detection, identification and classification of the threats. The chapter explains various types of access control systems, available sensors and detectors, video surveillance, remote monitoring of alarms and advance monitoring system.

Chapter 5 talks about new challenges being faced in industrial security like widespread civil disturbances, terrorist actions, major accidents, industrial espionage, bomb threats and nuclear hazards. Constant appraisal and reappraisal of the methods of meeting such threats is a dire necessity if the security function is to become meaningful and able to deliver the goods.

Chapter 6 explains Content and Process Theories of motivation. Content Theories are concerned with identifying what it is within an individual or the work environment that energize and sustain behaviour. Simply, what specific things motivate people? On the other hand, process theories try to explain and describe the process of how behaviour is energize, directed, and finally stopped. Better understanding of motivation thru a given set of tools will help managers responsible for safety and security to motivate employees and thus will help them to do their jobs better.

Chapter 7 presents an environmental systems model, which is derived from research on general systems theory. It is based on that fact that security is a dynamic process rather than as a static entity. The model examines the development of a security system through three phases; threat analysis, security system development and evaluation.

Chapter 8 briefs about Industrial security, its objectives, scope and the roles and responsibilities of various industrial security personnel.

Chapter 9 is about improving productivity, quality and performance in security and safety by three pronged approach of defining the task, concentrate work on the task and defining performance in quality and quantity. This approach will not only increase the productivity but will also increase the workers' self- respect and pride.

Chapter 10 talks about industrial policing and its limitations & hurdles in prevention of crime. The security personnel of a private industrial concern do not have any special powers or privileges as the police have for the performance of their duties, the law, however has bestowed certain limited rights and privileges on all citizens and they provide the necessary legal sanction for the different activities of the security personnel in the performance of their duty.

Chapter 11 shows the importance of people rather than technology, as the key for success in the workplace of the future. In tomorrow's workplace, emphasis will be on shared responsibility for group performance; jobs will be fluid and flexibility of paramount importance. Control will be shared and coordination will flow from shared goals and values; workers and managers will be partners. This also lists some new styles of motivating people.

Chapter 12 explains about a structured decision process for security design which considers the criticality of assets, the capabilities of potential threats, the likely outcome of attack attempts and the collective contribution of individual assets, facility and site protection strategies.

Chapter 13 takes a deep dive into security system design with creation of a security master plan as the first step. Other steps include threat and vulnerability analysis, security implications, design implications, schematic drawings and environmental design.

Chapter 14 describes about security surveys and how to carry out the surveys in your organization. Security survey is an assessment of the risk pertaining to a particular assignment. It highlights the particular physically security measures that are deemed necessary to lower or remove the risk factor on the assignment.

Chapter 15 touches upon the growing need of executive protection wherein large number of senior executives and high profile personalities are under threat from operatives who have developed worldwide ramifications through the nexus of terrorists, smugglers and gun runners. The chapter also provides interesting real-life case studies with lessons learnt from each of them.

Chapter 16 provides an interesting insight into how one can learn from his housewife about various management principles like how to manage boss, how to manage a difficult subordinate, and delegation, and professionalism, development of subordinates, motivation, happiness and authority.

Chapter 17 talks about the importance of softer aspects of the industrial security like creation of image of an effective security system in the industrial unit and the image projected by the security personnel thru his dressing (uniform), posture, stance, the style and content of communication.

We have also given elaborate recommendations of suggested readings and listed a number of books at the end of each chapter. I hope the articles in the book and also the suggested readings only make a useful and interesting reading for the banking security professionals, who are desirous to upgrade and update their knowledge and become an expert in security of banks. We propose to revised this book from time to time and bring out second edition of the book in the couple of years depending on the demand of readers. I will be happy and satisfied if this book has helped you in enhancing your knowledge base in any way and to improve your operational efficiency on the ground. I sincerely hope that this book will prove beneficial for the practising professionals.

Ravindra Singh

Editor & Executive Chairman, IISSM

Contributors

U K Chaubey

U K Chaubey joined public sector steel industry as a management trainee in 1960. In 1974, he joined Bharat Coking Coal Limited, a subsidiary of Coal India as Director (Personnel and Industrial Relations). He held important positions such as president of the National Institute of Personnel Management from 1991-93; vice president (Human Resource Management) in Hindalco Industries Limited. He has participated in a number of national and international seminars and has written papers on different aspects of Man Management.

Dr Arthur A Kingsbury

A Masters of Science in Police Administration, Dr Arthur A Kingsbury received his PhD from Wayne State University, USA. Currently, he is Associate Dean of Business, Health and Public Service at Macomb Community College. A former US Army Counter-Intelligence Officer, he has also studied British Intelligence Operations. At the International Institute of Safety and Security Management conference in 2000, the Governor of Karnataka presented him the IISSM Veteran of the Millennium Award. In March, 2002, he was selected as the Fulbright Scholar & Researcher to the Universidad de la Cordillera, La Paz, Bolivia.

Lauri A Kingsbury

Lauri A Kingsbury is a specialist in the field of Crime and Loss Prevention. She retired from the Crime Prevention Section of Detroit Police Department. A guest lecturer for the American Society of Industrial Security; Eastern Michigan University, Lambton College, Sarnia, Ontario; and Macomb Community College, Lauri has earned numerous awards and citations. She has written three text books for the Detroit Police Department. At present, she is the president of the Security Consulting Firm, Kingsbury & Kingsbury Limited.

Prof Renu Mattoo

Renu Mattoo is an English (Hons) Graduate from Delhi University and an alumna of XLRI, Jamshedpur, where she was awarded the Hindustan Lever Scholarship for obtaining the 1st rank and the Kumarappa and the Abdul Bari Gold Medals for overall academic excellence. She was on the faculty of XLRI, teaching core courses in Personnel Management apart from undertaking a number of in-company training and consultancy assignments for various companies. She is now an independent trainer-consultant offering programmes in leadership and confidence building.

Prof Sharu S Rangnekar

Sharu S Rangnekar is a chemical engineer from Bombay with a Masters of Business Administration degree from the USA. He carried out research work in Mathematical Economics at the Carnegie-Mellon University, Pittsburgh, USA. He had management training with Imperial Chemical Industries, UK and computer training with IBM and Union Carbide Corporation, USA. His books: "In the Wonderland of Indian Manager" and "In the World of Corporate Managers" have become management classics.

(Late) Sant Kumar Prasad Sinha

Masters in Political Science, Sant Kumar Prasad Sinha was Deputy Director Central Intelligence Bureau, Ministry of Home Affairs.

He had long experience of Industrial Security, Intelligence, Counter terrorism, Counter Espionage, Immigration. Sinha was recipient of Indian Police Medal for his contribution to the police service and a President's Police Medal for distinguished service. On his retirement in 1989, he joined SIS (I)and rose to the level of Executive Director (HQ). He retired on 31 October 2000.

Richard P Grassic
President, Techmark, Security Integration Services

R H Poole
He is managing director of Guard Defence Security Services Ltd. West Yorkshire, England

Katherin Xin
Katherin is a Research Associate with Graduate School of Management, University of California, USA

R K Srivastava, IPS
Inspector General
Central Industrial Security Force

Joginder Singh, IPS
Inspector General of Police
Central Reserve Police Force

Amulya Khurana
Amulya Khurana received her doctoral degree from IIT, Delhi. Her activities include teaching (Both UG and PG levels) and Research in Applied Psychology. Her areas of interest include Organizational Behaviour, HRM, Educational Psychology, Cognitive Psychology and Humanistic Psychology. She has authored one book and has contributed chapters in over eight books. Over 75 of her papers have been published and over 90 papers have been presented in various

national and international conferences. She has been a subject expert for a World Bank sponsored project: curriculum validation for Tribhuvan University, Kathmandu. She has also conducted a three day workshop at the same University on Research Methodolgy. She has completed a Research project, regarding effect of Vipassana Meditation, sponsored by Vipassana Research Institute.

Randy Atlas
Atlas Safety & Security Design Inc.

S M Wadekar
Wadekar is chief of the security in TELCO, Maharashtra

Industrial Security In India

Joginder Singh

India has the best industrial safety laws, which the human mind could conceive. If the same were to be implemented even to the extent of fifty percent, most of the industrial accidents would be a story of the past.

When it comes to the cutting corners, all savings are done only on the items which can be a security hazard.

In fact sometimes it is shocking to see that even the basic items like the gas extinguishers are not filled in time and the buckets for storing water for firefighting are used as dustbins.

During my visit to an undertaking as an officer in charge of the industrial security, in one of the state governments, I noted that the persons concerned with security did not know the telephone number of the city police control room or even the well- known fire warning number of 101. When I went into more details about the qualifications of the security staff, it was another sickening story. The persons who were not fit for any other active duty in the industry were given charge of security and fire fighting.

The private sector is perhaps the worst offender in this regard, well, with few exalted exceptions. The security staff particularly at the senior level is appointed only with a view to manage the industrial labor in the disputes between the labor and the managements or help the proprietors children in escaping the traffic violation. In fact one of the retired police officers who was appointed as chief of security told me personally that he had to spend more time in the police stations, sorting out the company problems rather than paying any attention to the job for which he was ostensibly appointed.

Though a number of gadgets have come into vogue like the close circuit TV, remote sensing devices or safety alarms, their use is not extensive and it is largely confined to the show rooms or in areas which can be a show piece for that particular industry. What is the solution?

One: The safety and security concepts should be part and parcel of all training programmes of the industry. In fact everybody should be told basics of fire fighting an industrial hazard and the matter not only left to the old decrepit *chowkidars,* who in some cases also double up as peons/ cooks and drivers. All industrial and management training programs should have the basics of industrial security as its integral component.

Two: One of the conditions of building and functioning of the Industry should be that it would spend at least ¼% of its total cost on taking steps for preventing and avoiding the industrial hazards, which should also include the security components as well as personnel in Industrial Security Modernization

Three: All MBA and other industrial courses for the top management should include sufficient briefing and instructions on the above subjects.

Four: All industries while organizing or sending its officers for any courses or refresher training programmes should emphasis on the organizer to include the subjects of the industrial security as an integral components.

Five: The entire staff should at least once a year be put through one day's refreshers course on fire fighting and anti- sabotaging drill.

Because this is job for which the whole industry has to be involved and not only a few chaps manning the gates of the parameters.

Ultimately the industry will find that by paying a little more emphasis on the above, it would be saving more than it would be spending but before that it has to get out the rut of treating the industrial security as another unnecessary, avoidable chore. Is the industry ready for this ? This can be answered by the industry only.

Motivating Security Personnel

Amulya Khurana

All security personnel are human beings and we therefore have to, go into the aspect of motivation of these security personnel as we would do for the employees. However, there are some special points which have been dealt, towards the end of this paper.

It is a well established fact that motivation and performance have a definite link. How to motivate the personnel, to do what needs to be done, has always been the concern of industries. After planning and organizing, the third function of a personnel manager is motivation. In order to make any managerial decision really meaningful, it is necessary to convert it into an effective action, which can be accomplished by motivating the employees. To motivate means to produce goal–oriented behaviour. Since important function of the management. Almost every aspect of the personnel function in pervasively endowed with motivational attributes. (Tripatin, 1985)

Human motives are based on needs. These needs may be consciously or subconsciously felt and vary in intensity over time with various individuals. Needs constitute first set of variables.

"Motivation, in a general term apply to the entire class of drive, desires, needs, wishes and similar forces. To say that managers motivate their subordinates is to say that they do these things which they hope will safely use these drivers and desires and induce the subordinates to act in a desired manner.(Koontz& O'Donnell 1978).

When one talks about character, what the individual does in the work situation, constitutes the second set of variables. Primarily this means what he does on his job are the characteristics of the job. As Hawthorne studies show, job – connected experience of a worker plays an important part in determining his motivation. Organization structure, technological systems, physical facilities, etc, are some parameters that are more motivating than others.

The third set of variable come under what happens to the individual in the work situation, namely the characteristics of the immediate work environment, particularly the attitudes and actions of supervisors and peers and characteristics of the organizations actions.

In addition, certain exogenous variables such as customs and norms, images and attributes conferred by society about motivation. One can also talk about what energies persons behavior, what directs it, and what maintains and sustains it. Motivation involves a chain reaction – starting out with felt needs, resulting in wants or goals sought, which gives rise to tensions (that in unfulfilled desires) then causing action towards achieving goals, and finally satisfying wants. However, motivation is not as simple as it seems to be. It is a highly complex phenomenon and it is difficult to pinpoint one single strategy to all people and in every situation equally. There are three major sets of variables that are most critical for understanding how the motivational process operates in organizational settings. Motivation is the result of interplay among these groups of factors:

1. Influences operating within the individual.

To understand what motivates an employee, it is imperative to know what he brings to the work situation, that is the characteristic of the individual : his interests, attitudes, needs, aims and values. Human needs are both numerous and complex. Some of these are hard to describes and identify because the real needs are hidden beneath an overlay acceptable behaviors, by the individual.

2. Like leadership

Motivation is also highly situational, particular jobs are occupations and the workers home life- all play a strong motivational role. An individual may find his work substantial degree of respect and social acceptance accorded by society which is quite apart from holding a position in a particular organization. These are some of the determinants of motivation. However, knowledge of these motivational determinants is not a magic key to motivate people. Peterson (1978) has pointed out some of the influences that help to create employee attitudes – those influences which can be applied consciously and those over which one has little or no control. These influences help or shape the employees decision concerning how he or she will work. The workers make this decision which managements cannot. Often, managements definitions of policy influences the employees, in making the decision. Management cannot force employees to work efficiently but it can set a stage through its policies where it is easier for them to decide to work efficiently.

All that management can do is to identify the influences over which it has no control and extend its influence wherever possible. Some of these influences are :

The influence of the attitudes of the group toward productivity.
Although each employee is an individual, he or she is also an integral part or a member of a group. Each group has a distinct personality of its own and makes decision. it sets its own goals, which may or may not be identical with managements goals. Each group set its own mortal standards.

The influence of selection and placement.
This is very basic control that has in recent years become increasingly

difficult to utilize. Government today has a large amount of control over the process and some industries have almost given up control in this area. The selection process involves : (1) biographical data through applications, interviews, reference and other sources and (2) tests such as physical examination qualification defects skills tests, job knowledge tests knowledge tests and psychological tests.

The influence of training.

Training is a powerful influence and motivator in productivity, just as it is in many others area. In training employees, you give them only two things- knowledge and skill. You get three things in return –knowledge, skill and motivation. This has been shown over and over again in business. Industry today is engaged in more training than ever before in history.

Training is however often terribly misused, it is too often considered a panacea for problems in industry. More often than not, management perceives a performance problem and, without diagnosing the problem, decides that some training is needed, when, the problem may actually be in poor procedures, poor selection, or poor management etc.

Training is effective when it is aimed at defined needs when analysis shows the problems to be lack of skill, or even lack of motivation. It is waste of time when the problem is elsewhere in the system. Management must give due consideration on how to train, whom and when to train and what to provide in training.

The influence of supervision.

Everything that motivates employees is applied by the supervisor and obviously this role is crucial. The supervisor, of course, must be motivated and must share the company's goals in order to achieve the purpose of motivating the employees.

The influence of special emphasis program.

A special emphasis program is not just a gimmick. It is a coordinated campaign aimed at a defined problem. A well-run and well-developed special emphasis program can exert an important influence on employees.

The influence of media.

Media are not without value. They are extremely valuable but only when heard by receptive ears and seen by receptive eyes. The individual must be motivated to utilize media properly, media does not motivate by themselves.

Motivational refers to the drive and effort to satisfy a want or goal. Satisfaction refers to the contentment experienced when a want in satisfied. In other words motivation implies a drive towards an outcome and satisfaction, involves outcomes already experienced. (Koontz &o' Donnell, 1978) Philosophers and scientists have been trying to define the relationship between work and need satisfaction. KARL MARX (1963) explained the relationship between work and need satisfaction as : work is not the satisfaction of a need but a means of satisfying other needs. This implies that man works so that his needs may be satisfied. However, Dunnell (1967) observed that many jobs, in both manufacturing units and offices are poor motivators as measured against persons list of needs.

The current search for excellence and the increasing emphasis on quality is reflected in the effort to identity and study the motivational determinants of employees in the work environment (Cunnings & Elsalmi, 1968) Motivators are those factors, which induce an individual to perform. They may include higher pay, prestige title, a name on the officer door, the acclaim of colleagues and host of other things that give people a reason to perform. To be sure, while motivators reflects wants, they offer rewards or incentives, that sharpen the drive to satisfy these wants, they are also the means by which conflicting needs may be reconciled or ones need heightened so that it will be given priority over another. A motivator is something that influences an individual's behavior. It makes a difference in what a person will do.

Despite all the researches and theories of motivation that have come to fore in recent years, rewards and punishments are still strong motivators. The incentives which are frequently offered to the workers include pay and others types of rewards and fringe benefits. On the other hand are negative incentives of punishments and reprimands. Different rewards related to specific job hold different incentives values for the workers. (Dwivedi, 1979). Several studies have been conducted in India on the relative importance of different rewards for industrial workers, Sinhan (1970) has summarized the results of these studies. Some studies are exploratory which analyses the incentives which influence Indian workers and determine their relative strength. Ganguli (1954) showed that the three most highly ranked incentives are : adequate earning, job security and opportunity for promotion. Bhatt (1962) conducted three studies which showed that out of nine incentives, choice of work, advancement and co-workers were ranked first, second and third respectively wages ranked fourth while the fifth place was a tie between benefits and condition of work and the supervisors. The last three in priority were security, hours of works and holidays respectively. These exploratory studies have provided confusing results.

The security personnel deserve a very special treatment due to inherent risk involved their job. Their perks must be really attractive, their family security must be guaranteed by the industrial organizations. They must have extra promotional avenues and due recognition. In order to instill confidence. They must be imparted a very intensive and high degree of training. In short, given proper motivation, there in nothing a man cannot do. The following model proposes that there in a joint effect of various sets factors on the motivational of security personnel.

Role of Intelligence in Industrial Security

S K P Sinha

Security means safety and for ensuring safety a security system is devised. The system so devised, be it for national security or for security of an individual or an establishment, has to be an integrated system of which intelligence is an important component.

Intelligence provides knowledge of the forces endangering or likely to end safety and without this knowledge no security system can function. Intelligence assesses and evaluates the strength and resources of the forces inimical and without this information no security system can be formulated, nor can it be made cost effective, designing of physical barriers, placing of sophisticated electronic gadgets, deployment of security guards, etc. all depend on an evaluation of threat which intelligence only can provide.

Mentioning in general, security of an industrial establishment faces threats from several corners. At one corner is the lurking burglar waiting for an opportune time, at another is the trade unionist aiming at the throat of the management. At other corners are the contractors turned mafia fleecing the concern, disgruntled cum militant employees awaiting to be avenged, emotionally surcharged youths turned terrorists trying to show by staging some spectacular action . Thus, depending upon its threat perception and vulnerability an industrial security system, many have to look for one or more of the following intelligence back up.

1. Criminal Intelligence

Almost all industrial establishments are vulnerable to thefts and pilferage. Thefts may be of raw materials or of finished products or of fittings and fixtures. Machineries and machine parts may also be stolen. Scraps and saleable commodities in slag dumps too may not be spared.

Things are stolen or pilfered from inside the campus or while they are in transit with or without the connivance of the transporters. Many thefts go undetected, some are not even reported or recorded. Loss suffered by an establishment on account of all these thefts and pilferages often are too heavy.

Things are stolen because they have a ready market in the vicinity. Agents also operate who motivate indigents for thefts, and it is often seen that some persons around an establishment become rich in no time. Organized gangs also operate for higher stakes.

The problem cannot be tackled by deployment of guards alone. They can physically prevent if any theft is taking place before their eyes, but the task of identifying the gang or the receiver of stolen goods and working out any case or finding out the culprits are beyond their means and can be shouldered only by a team of intelligence men, well trained in tracking and preventing crimes. This team can also take up other types of crimes, if any, committed inside the establishment. Close liaison with the police and the administration can be the other responsibility of this team.

2. Labour intelligence

Healthy and constructive trade unionism is welcome. But in India unfortunately trade unionism by large is destructive and often a big obstacle in the growth of an industry. Many of the industries suffer from multiplicity of trade unions, each warning against other and promoting indiscipline and disloyalty among the employees. Their inter and intra union rivalries cause even killings, resulting in an atmosphere of mutual hatred and animosity. Strikes and intimidation as also incidents of assaults on executives are almost a daily feature and the moment one tries to enforce some work culture, he is pressurized and cowed down.

It is true that some establishments have laudable industrial relations, but when the entire atmosphere is vicious and becoming poisoned more and more every day, it is doubtful as to how long the honeymoon will last. Labour lawlessness is becoming the order of the day and though today it is not here, tomorrow it is bound to be here too.

One obviously cannot change the climate, but he can at least know as to how the climate is going to affect his house. He can get forewarned and may use the knowledge to devise suitable technique for countering the oncoming threat. An eye over the labour force and their unions is, therefore necessary and since it is an everyday job, a team of suitably trained intelligence operatives is imperative for an industrial establishment which wants to grow in peace. This team may also have a general watch over the developing political situation in the area as a watch on Indian trade unions cannot be meaningful without keeping an eye on Indian political parties.

3. Counter intelligence

There may also be occasions when some counter intelligence work appears necessary in respect of those who may be collecting information, tactical or strategically for some ulterior motive. The motive may be to harm the nation or the establishment. Plans of mischief or subversion or even sabotage may be there, and for unearthing that a counter – intelligence outfit is necessary. Inimical and hostile foreign powers do collect intelligence of various types including that of industrial health which provides an insight into the nation's economic health. And this is very vital for any inimical design for subversion or subjugation. The trust to safeguard the nation from this danger is very sacred and you have to fulfill it with all the responsibility. Foreign collaborators or technicians may be with you but then you must have suitable means to know what they do in their spare time. Suitable means with you will be only a countered intelligence wing if you have.

Commercial intelligence is also collected by some interested agencies located inside and outside the country. Subtle efforts to take over are also there, and unless forewarned and countered in time, recovery may not be possible. The work, involved in this regard is not a counter intelligence work in the normal sense as we understand. But with the necessary briefing and training and a programme specifically designed for the purpose, the counter intelligence wing can be entrusted with this responsibility also.

Information leakage to a competing or hostile concern is another problem. Leakages have to be plugged and for that adequate measures are to be taken. The measures include physical security, security of documents, security of personnel etc, and the counter intelligence wing can undertake the responsibility for devising the details and also monitoring their implementation.

4. Intelligence for Executive Protection

Tentacles of terrorism are not confined to government officers and political leaders. Sector business executives of both public and private sectors are now becoming the targets of terrorists. Terrorists want publicity and business executives attract publicity of the same level as that of the government officers and political leaders. The choice also becomes easier when the security cordon around a target is weak which normally the case with business executives.

And there are disgruntled employees, who are not terrorists but may like to act like terrorists in order to take revenge and satisfy their ego. Contractors turned mafia may also have scores to settle. Thus, in view of the increasing vulnerability of business executives to terrorist and terrorist like threats, the executive protection wing of the establishment needs some intelligence back up in order to identify and specify the threat and also to devise measures for countering them.

5. Vigilance

We have talked a lot about outside forces and now it is time for us to look inwards. Dangers or threats to security or safety emanate from both outside and inside forces. For a house if a coat of plaster is essential from outside, a similar coat is also need from inside. In fact, threats from inside are more serious and dangerous so we should not neglect threats generating or brewing inside.

Such a state of affairs is apparent from the fact that very few establishments get their executives vetted before their appointments. I do not mean the same type of vetting as the government does, but vetting on the points relevant, like honesty, integrity, loyalty, work, attitude etc. is a must. Shifting from one establishment to another is more frequent among the executives of industrial concerns and vetting of antecedents in such cases becomes more important, as it must be known whether the proposed shifting is just for better prospects or for some other reason.

Periodical vetting in some selective cases is also recommended for those who handle sensitive information or hold post in which some additional money can be earned just by closing an eye. Discreet watch at times in such cases may also be necessary. There may also be occasions to substantiate a charge sheet by a regular enquiry and for such enquires the vigilance team would be handy.

The intelligence task and responsibility of an integrated security system of an industrial establishment have been outlined in brief. Now, I would like to invite your attention to some general problems which intelligence operative face in an industrial set up.

The first problem is of anonymity of intelligence imperative. Barring a few of them engaged in criminal intelligence, the bulk shouldering other responsibilities like vigilance, counter intelligence etc. should not be known, as the moment their identify becomes known they become outcasts and lose their usefulness. They also fall prey to human weakness of bragging and corruption. It is, therefore, suggested that as far as possible some convenient spots in the normal set up may be created for absorbing such intelligence operatives who require anonymity. Care should also be taken that the work assigned to them in the office or elsewhere is not very heavy defeating the very purpose of having them. Slots convenient to them may be found in the departments of personnel, reception, liaison, public relation, telephones, sanitation etc.

Suitable persons already employed in the establishment may also be used as intelligence operatives after imparting them accessory training. This is however a long term measure. A via media is therefore, suggested and that is we may have a mixture of both the types, while the trained and experienced operatives may have convenient slots, others utilized casually or at times may be selected and picked up from among the existing employees. The necessary training may be imparted to them with due discretion by the trained and experienced operatives who select them.

Another problem which an intelligence outfit faces is its command and control. Normally the chief who also incidentally becomes the chief of security, reports to the chief of the establishment. However, due to latter's preoccupations the work is often delegated to this 21/C. As long as this practice is there, there is no problem, but the delegation should not, in any case, go down the level of 21/C, of the establishment. The danger in delegating the command and control to lower functionaries is that the importance of the tasks assigned to the intelligence gets eroded and the tendency to get away with a wishy-washy report develops. There also is the risk of exposure of men and leakage of information and that must be avoided at all cost.

Gentlemen, security is safety and safety ensures growth and profitability. Unfortunately priority accorded to security in many of the industrial establishments is very low. Intelligence receives even a lower priority. This problem must be looked into urgently as any rupee saved now may cost you, thousands in due course. The misgiving that security including intelligence is not an earning section may please be avoided as we all know that without safety nothing prospers and it is only an integrated security earning section. However, its earning are indirect and not noticeable.

The intention is, however, not to create a leviathan in the name of security or intelligence. Man power and resources have to be need based and requirements worked out with the help of experts.

Equipment Support for Identification of Security Threats

R K Sinha

Increasing unemployment, socio-economic problems, general deterioration in law & order situation and ever increasing terrorism and violence all over the world has increased security threats to industries and institutions.

Security threats to high value asset areas are on the increase to industries world-wide and it is a misconception that security threats to the industries in India and other developing countries are more.

Due to sophistication of modus operandi of the criminals, it has become imperative that security threat assessment, identification, classification and response is made perfect and that minimum time is lost in this process.

Objective of this Workshop

The objective of this presentation will be to:

I. Identify major threats to the security of industries in India;

II. To share experience and knowledge of available equipment and gadgets;

III. To recommend an ideal mix of manpower and equipment for

- Reduction in threat probabilities;
- Ensuring faster and effective communication to the reaction force.

Benefits of Equipment Installations

Any security problem has following main ingredients;

- Threat vulnerability;
- Identification of the threat;
- Classification of the threat;
- Communication of the threat signals;
- Reaction to the threat

Primary Detection Components Primary Detection Components lies in discovery, by the protective force of an adversary action. Threat vulnerability mainly depends on the value of the assets and degree of accessibility, however threat vulnerability will differ from industry to industry depending on how difficult it is to reach to the assets and what is the possible risk of apprehension in the process. If the accessibility is easier and risks of apprehensions are negligible – vulnerability will increase. But, if the access becomes difficult and danger of apprehension in the process is increased, vulnerability will decrease considerably. The major benefit of installation of equipment and gadgets in security is to ensure that access to valuable assets is made as difficult as possible and the probability of identification and apprehension of criminals is maximized.

Access Control

The first key to security of industries is to have a very rigid, efficient and effective system of access control. The ideal system of access control must ensure that.

(a) Access to the industry premises is NOT uncontrolled;

(b) When an entry is granted to a customer, a visitor or an employee within the bank premises, there must be a system of identification, classification and recording in case of each entry

(c) System of access control must ensure that even within the premises, a second check is exercised before permitting entry to high value asset areas, like managers cabin, computer room etc.

The following types of access control systems are available in the market today-

- Turnstile gate;
- Keypad code access;
- Micro processor card reader;
- Computerized video image processor;
    a. Photo matching
    b. Eye retina matching
    c. Signature matching
    d. Finger print matching
- Combination of more than one for high risk areas

Available Sensors & Detectors

A number of sensors and detectors are available in the market today. Prominent amongst those are;-

- Microwave sensors;
- Ultrasonic sensors;
- Passive infrared sensors;
- Capacitance proximity detectors;
- Vibration sensors;
- Magnetic switch type sensors;
- Glass break sensors;
- Photoelectric beam sensors;
- Pressure mat sensors

Common purpose of all types of sensors is to detect:

- Energy
- Motion
- Sound
- Vibration
- Heat

- Capacitance;
- Pressure;
- Light

Microwave Sensors: Microwave sensors are motion detector sensors that broadcasts signals in a protected area and monitors changes to those signals caused by an intruder. The advantages of microwave sensors are that it covers a wide range and can penetrate some construction materials also.

Ultrasonic Sensors: The ultrasonic sensors are also motion detector sensors which broadcast a signal into a protected area and monitors that signal for changes caused by an intruder.

Passive Infrared Sensor: Passive infrared sensors are motion detector sensors that can sense the difference between background infrared energy and the energy level of an intruder and sets off an alarm when an intruder enters within its range. The PIR sensors are available in many different patterns to suit virtually any requirement. It can be wall mounted, roof mounted, step focused or available in any other configuration

Capacitance Proximity Detectors: Capacitance proximity detectors are point sensors which detect changes in capacitance of metallic objects and ground. Objects to be protected must be insulated from the ground to eliminate possible errors.

A single capacitance detector can detect any threat from 60 to 75 filing cabinets, safes or desks.

Vibration Sensors: Vibration sensors are generally of two types;

(i) Mechanical type vibration sensors which detect movement of a mass or weight when opened and closed in a set of contacts; and

(ii) Electrical type devices sense vibrations passing through structural materials. Vibration sensors are commonly used in walls, ceilings, metal cages and safes & vaults.

Magnetic Switch Type Sensors: Magnetic switch type sensors are one of the oldest, simplest, most reliable, dependable, commonly available and widely used sensors. Magnetic/Balanced Magnetic switch type sensors basically protect movable openings, like doors, windows, ventilators, roofs, hatches etc.

Magnetic sensors are available in various configurations including surface mount, recessed, special purpose, overhead doors, windows, gates, explosion-proof, armored cars, cash vaults etc.

Warning: While magnetic sensors are simple, fool-proof sensors for detecting opening of a protected door and window, it will not detect cutting of the door or other type of penetrations without opening the magnetic contacts.

Glass Break Sensors: Glass break sensors are also special type of motion and sound detecting sensors which are generally of two types:

- Contact type devices which are mounted on a glass or adjacent to the glass and detect the shock, stress and vibration associated with the glass breakage.
- Audio type glass break sensors which detect the exact type of sound of breaking of glass.

There are dual technology glass break sensors also available which combine both detection of vibration and sound. In dual type glass break sensors alarm will be generated after detection of both vibration and sound. Therefore, it will reduce NAR (Nuisance Alarm Ratio) caused by environmental reasons.

Glass break sensors are very popular for windows, display cases, ventilators, cash windows etc. Use of these type of sensors is on increase world- wide with increase in use of glass as a common substitute of wooden panels of doors and window.

Warning: Glass break sensors are not effective in the protection of special type of glass, like tempered glass, some kinds of tinted glasses, safety glass, or glass substitute. Therefore, it is advised to keep this factor in mind while ordering glass installations.

Photoelectric Beam Sensors: Photoelectric Beam Sensors are detection devices that generates an alarm when the photoelectric beam is broken. These kind of sensors are available in many configurations including long range photoelectric beam sensors and miniature photoelectric sensors. The advantage of these type of sensors are that photoelectic beams are not visible to the naked eye unless special spectacles are used to identify them. Photoelectric beam sensors are very useful for long corridors, doorways, long rows of windows, aisles going to the high value asset areas like cash vaults and locker rooms.

Pressure Mat Sensors: It is a trap type sensor which is installed underneath carpeting or flooring. It detects the pressure of an intruder walking on the captured surface very efficiently. Since it is very difficult for an intruder to determine the presence or location, it can be effectively used at entry point to the vulnerable areas like windows, staircase and underneath.

Performance Characteristics

There are 3 major performance characteristics namely:

PD or Probability of detection: This means likelihood of detecting an adversary with in a zone covered by the sensors.

NAR or Nuisance Alarm Rate: It is an alarm not attributed to the adversary action, but caused by different environmental factors. NAR is normally common in exterior sensors like fence sensors, wired sensors, cable sensors etc. which is not of much relevance in security of building premises like a bank.

FAR or False Alarm Rate: This means the expected rate of alarm which are neither attributed to adversary activities nor caused due to environmental reasons. Causes of most of the FAR are unknown and can be due to the fault of equipment and circuits.

Major Problems: Vulnerability to defeat: Adversaries are known to counter the efforts of detection & try to by-pass or spoof the range of the sensors. Therefore, the ideal detection technique to reduce the VD (Vulnerability to defeat) and to increase PD (Probability of detection), dual technology sensors are becoming increasingly popular.

Dual technology sensors means, sensors working on two technologies available in the same housing. Primary purpose of using the dual technology sensor is to reduce NAR (Nuisance Alarm Rate). Some of the popular combinations are:

- PIR + Microwave
- Audio + Mechanical Glass break
- Microwave + Photoelectric.

However, it is recommended to cover high value asset areas by maximum type of sensors to increase PD and to reduce NAR, FAR, and VD.

Future Generation Sensors: The research and development in the field of alarms and sensors is continuing with following objectives in mind:

- To improve signal processing.
- To improve probabilities of detectors.
- To reduce Nuisance Alarms and False Alarms.
- To miniaturize sensors.
- To make on and off remote.

Some of current R & D has given positive results in developing sensors described as under:-

- Fiber Optic
- Piezo Film
- Terrain Following Microwave
- Strain Gauge / Load Cell
- Air Space Monitoring
- Early warning Detector

Video Surveillance

Video surveillance is becoming more and more popular and useful in detection and recording of intruder's activities. As the identification of the threat is audio visual and precise; it improves quality of reaction in terms of reaction time and preparedness. Video surveillance has following distinguished advantages:-

- Precision in identification of threat;
- Option of video recording with on / off button or automatically due to activation of an alarm.
- Miniature cameras and resolution night vision cameras.
- Pan & Tilt and Ceiling Dome cameras.

Remote Monitoring of Alarms

Most of rural and semi-urban banks in India are handicapped with limited reaction force to meet any security threat., The major problems in most of such banks are to mobilize the effective reaction force in time in case of any threat. Therefore, it is equally important for the bank to effectively transmit the threat signal outside the bank premises to a place from where reinforcement can be expected such as nearest Police Station, Fire Station, Security, Control Rooms, Superior functionaries of the banks, nearest another branch etc. This is applicable to many industries and even residential houses.

Lately it has been observed that armed robbers have violently reacted to the sound of alarms and even to the slight resistance from the employees. As such, now a days, employees normally would not dare to activate an alarm and in turn create a threat to their own lives. Therefore, it has become necessary that signals of the alarms generated by activation of a detector or sensors or by activation by a manual switch is monitored from a remote place.

Latest developments have made available various kinds of remote communications/ monitoring systems. A few important systems are as under-

Silent Communicator: This is a small communication unit interfaced with a telephone line on the one end and to the various sensors and detectors on the other end. The moment any of the sensors and detectors detect a potential security thereat it activates an alarm, the silent communicator is automatically activated and by using the telephone line silently dials up to 10 numbers and communicates a pre-recorded threat message. Disadvantages of silent communicator are:

- Does not work when telephone line is out of order or damaged.
- Not capable of classifying the threat.

Advantages of silent communicator are:

- It has low cost and is an easily available item and can be interfaced with any type of sensors or alarms.

Integrated Monitoring System: There are various kinds of integrated alarms and sensors available, which monitor the signal received from within the building. All these systems function on the principle of converting various kinds of signals received from the sensors into telephone communication signals and carrying these through the users' telephone line to a signal-processing unit, which identifies and classifies the nature of threat and alarms reaction forces accordingly.

This kind of integrated alarm monitoring system has prevented thousands of bank robberies and theft in Europe and America in past few years and have resulted into interception of criminals while committing the crime in majority of the cases.

(i) Advance Monitoring System: There is recent advancement in centralised remote monitoring systems having following additional advantages; Voice recognition and recording- With this, it is possible to not only identify and classify the threat at a location, but also to hear the exact sound generated at the place of occurrence including conversation and it is possible to record these conversations.

(ii) Scrambling of signals: Now-a-days it is possible to scramble the out-going signals and again de-scramble it at the Control Station. This ensures protection from interception of signals and also ensures speedy communication of the signal to the control station.

(iii) Wireless Transmission: It is also possible to interface radio communication unit at each location, which will transmit the signal on radio frequency after scrambling to the control station. The additional advantage of this system is that is does not have to depend on the telephone lines. However, this system is quite expensive even in Western Countries.

CONCLUSION

I would like to conclude this with the following remarks:-

- To provide an effective counter to the increasing challenges to the security of industries in India, there is no option except to use latest equipments for detection, identification and classification of the threats.

- A fully secured atmosphere will ensure a better working culture and efficiency.

Fibre Optic Systems for Perimeter Control

R K Srivastava

Industrial security is gradually taking up a bigger role, Apart from meeting the usual threats of thefts, pilferages, trespass and management- employee disputes, some new threats have emerged which necessitate consideration and analysis. Some of these new challenges which have to be faced squarely are widespread civil disturbances, terrorist actions, major accidents, industrial espionage, bomb threats and nuclear hazards. One or all can be expected in the more vital industries like petroleum and petro-chemical atomic energy, thermal power, heavy industries and drugs. Constant appraisal and reappraisal of the methods of meeting such threats is a dire necessity if the security function is to become meaningful and able to deliver the goods.

Wide-spread Civil Disturbances

The wide spread communal disturbances in Northern India after the assassination of Indira Gandhi tested the resources and capabilities of those responsible for security, not only in the police sphere but also in the industrial areas. While emergency plans had been drawn up in many undertakings, they had not envisaged the type of situations that unfolded when passions got amused on a mass scale within the undertaking and the residential colonies attached to them. In some areas there was no clear demarcation between residential areas and the undertaking working areas, the problem was further computed for the security personal. Greater emphasis had to be laid on the collection of intelligence, guarding of the members of the minority community and their work areas, protection of the plant property and last but not least, closer and constant supervision by the senior officers. Greater and frequent liaison with the local police authorities has to be made and would be required again in case of any similar or other kind of civil disturbance in future in order to ensure harmony in the plant areas and nearby. Above all the role of intelligence collection would have to redefined and higher degree of initiative and drive from the supervisory and subordinate officers would have to be insisted upon and performances careful reviewed and analysed.

Terrorist Action

The most potent threat to industrial security in the present times is posted by terrorists and organisations which believe in the cull of violence to achieve political or politico—religious ends. The continuing spate of assassinations and other violent acts within country brings out fact that the capacity for offensive item rest with the terrorists are able to seal off their organisation effectively which indicates a high degree of motivation, training and the existence of a base of sympathisers who are able to provide them rest and recuperation. Industrial undertakings particularly, those engaged in hazardous operations are especially susceptible to the terrorist threats.

A reorientation is perhaps called for in training and motivation of security personnel as also the intelligence network which is appended with the security units. Higher level of planning and anticipation of possible strikes by terrorist is also required at the supervisory level. Some form of awareness of the hazards and dangers posed by such elements also need to be brought about among the workers in the various industrial undertaking so that effort of the security to anticipate and meet the challenge are supplemented by those for whom the entire exercise has been undertaken. Some restructuring of the security forces at the macro level is also imperative. Quick Reaction Groups are needed in especially sensitive undertaking to prevent and engage suddenly take over's, assaults and commando type attacks by terrorist group. New lists of physical defensive measures which need to put up should be insisted upon in the industrial undertakings for implementation along with the other security measures. Increasing use of technical gadgets also need to be stressed upon.

Major Accidents

Occurrences like the Bhopal gas tragedy, sulphuric acid leakage at the DCM chemicals works in Delhi and liquid ammonium gas spillage in the Rashtriya Chemical and Fertilizers storage yard at Bombay have posed a different kind of challenge to security. Accident prevention is not strictly speaking a security function but the enforcement of rules and regulations pertaining to them is, and the aftermath of such accidents, role of security and more so when it is located in or near an urban setting becomes important. The emergency or internal disaster plans which are currently drawn up according to a standard pattern need to be re—examined in the light of some of the recent disasters. And the shortcomings in the schemes need rectification if not complete change. Such plans must cater for:

(a) assignment of personnel to specific tasks and responsibilities,
(b) expanding and simplifying instructions relating to the use of alarm system and signals,
(c) quicker dissemination and information concerning methods contained of dangers by fire and other pollutants,
(d) devising of system for notification of appropriate persons more speedily,
(e) round the clock dissemination of information of information concerning location of relief equipment to all,

(f) specification of evacuation routes and other procedures and,
(g) drawing up other provisions as the local situation may demand.

It is not sufficient to merely draw up an emergency or a disaster plan and propagate its provisions to personnel by posting throughout the undertaking. Drills must be held regularly at least once each quarter for each of the basic shifts under varied conditions. This would ensure that all personnel on all the kinds of duty are trained to perform assigned tasks and make them familiar with the use of operation of the various types of safety equipment. Last but not least evaluation of the effectiveness of the plan itself should be carried at frequent intervals.

Planning foe any types of emergency or accident requires close liaison with other neighbouring authorities. Security administration must meet and liaise with such authorities regularly for mutual planning and performance.

Industrial Espionage

As technology develops and undertaking start competing with front line technologies, espionage in the industrial areas is likely to emerge as a serious challenge. New methods of access control would also be needed to check unauthorised visitors and trespassers. Here the use of new and more sophisticated scientific grudges cannot be over emphasised. The existing system of identification by way of identity cards (laminated or otherwise) would not meet the purpose. The most important part of any security arrangement being the intelligence set up it would need to be updated to pre-exempt any thereat of the type discussed above.

Bomb Threats

Bombs and bomb threats are serious problems in the offing for many industries and institutions. Typically a telephone call is received from an unknown source stating that a bomb has been planted in the building. Advanced planning is required to handle such incidents properly. Liaison with the local, state or provincial police can be of great assistance in such planning. Recommendations by them or authorities concerned with such matters should apply to all undertakings. Specialised training is necessary for handling of such threats, search of the premises, evacuation of workers, sealing off of the affected areas, termination of the threat and analysis and review. Where bomb—threats are indicative of a future event, access control would need to be tightened and decisions taken on whether or not property or goods being brought into the undertaking would be examined thoroughly. Here again the role of security gadgets like x-ray machines, sniffers and metal detectors cannot be over—emphasised.

Nuclear Hazards

The accidents at Chernobyl in Russia were a unique form of hazards for which the security and other agencies proved to be quite unprepared. Despite the claims that such accidents, cannot and will not occur in this country, it is imperative that those concerned with the security of such establishments should constantly monitor their state of preparedness, and availability of physical defences like protective clothing and special detection devises, medical facilities and backup relief measures. A close look would also be required at the equipment of security personal evolved, and testing of their knowledge of the various plant processes ensured. Only with a higher degree of understanding of the actual working of the plant would the security function become meaningful and effective in such crises.

In the ultimate analysis, the preparations for meeting any kind of challenge of security require concentration in 3 major areas –training, intelligence collection and provision of scientific equipment.

While the existing system of paramilitary training is adequate enough for meeting threats posed by ordinary criminals, it is not potent to meet the emerging special challenges. A higher degree of educational achievement and educational achievement, motivation and technical expertise needs to be suitably incorporated in the training syllabi. In the matter of intelligence collection a distinction has to be made between information gathering and collection of hard intelligence. The time has perhaps come to adopt more aggressive forms of intelligence gathering in view of the threats posed by the terrorists and other similar elements. Separate cells for shifting and analysing intelligence are necessary in every security set up apart from the field staff. Training in the operation and maintained of scientific security gadgets is another area which needs immediate attention and highest priority. The progress made in other countries in this regard needs to be monitored closely and made supplementary to the research and evaluation programmes undertaken by the security set ups. The time may well come when gadgetry and its evolutionary forms would almost replace the human element.

Fibre Optic Systems for Perimeter Control

The application of fibre optics abroad in security equipment and installations is gaining ground with large scale benefits in the industry and other end—customers. A wide range of option is available with regard to the systems devised and available for budget, thus achieving perimeter security. Specific systems can be devised to meet any particular threat or conform to a specified budget, thus achieving a high rate of cost effectiveness. Installation, repair and maintained techniques for fibre optic systems have been simplified. Standard connections are now available and high grade skills are not required to install even the most sophisticated system.

Some of the recent applications are in the field of guarding Railway sidings, Oil Refiners, Power Plants, Defence installations and prisons. Fibre Optic Systems are immune from disturbances caused in other electronic equipment by moving objects, electrical equipment in the vicinity, vibrations, weathers changes like humidity, higher winds, dust, ball rain etc. Disturbances baby wind borne litter, small animals, falling leaves and snow do not affect the working of those systems like they do in the case of CCTV systems, volumetric and proximity sensors, which normally fail or give false alarms.

Another advantage in the use of Fibre Optic Security systems for potential users is the easy and adequate availability of world wide support by the manufactures. Technical support, literature, training packages and installation techniques are now readily available, reliable to accept, follow and implement. Any security system, big or small, can be easily designed, fabricated and installed with options to make any number of modifications subsequently.

For perimeter security, the best use is salve tape material which is a serrated tape containing an optical fibre. It can be attached to fences and configured in such a way that any attempt to force a passage through it will trigger an alarm. The system can also be installed to present an anti climb on trigger arrangement. This prevents climbers from gaining access to flat roofs or higher elevations of buildings and also presents in effective barriers to climbers, whether moving over walls or fences. The on trigger also contains a shear fibre which is broken if a climber brings weight to bear on any of the support metal work.

Other techniques for perimeters security are available using the same principal. The fibre optic can be disguised as a strainer and clipped to regions of chain link or wield mesh fencing. When intruder attempts to lift the bottom of the fence for gaining access the fibre optic breaks and activates an alarm. Fibre Optic can be contained in flexible sleeves, Kevlar reinforced if necessary as in the case of proximity sensing wires. Use of noise free fibre optic communications can help in bringing zone by zone information to a Central Control Room. The efficiency can be further enhanced for perimeter security by using such fibre optic sensors interactively with CCTV or other electronic sensors.

In addition to their use in barbed metal/type, optical fibres can be woven into meshes, to create fibre optic nets which can be used as security sensors around highly guarded zones. These meshes can also be deployed as cladding material inside walls, around perimeters or under water. It can be manufactured in precise panel shapes; where each panel can be zone to enable systems designers, architects and security installation companies to access flexible security sensors. Kevlar reinforcing of the Fibre Optic cable in such meshes gives them structural strength.

Existing structures can get enhanced protection by use of fibre optic panels and specially shaped cladding material. They can also be used in equipment to detect attempts to deglaze for example roof lights where by optical fibres are run through buttons bounded in the glass advancement to the glazing bars.

While the application of fibre optics in security equipment realise on the fibre being broken to activate an alarm it is possible to apply them in systems which can signal an alarm without breaking them. In date transmission, security equipment it can be arranged to place a security signal over the date signal by using fibre optics.

The physical principals of fibre optics are simple and easily understood. They are made from glass or polymer that is strong, flexible and can be configured in a wide variety of devices. In communications, this signal is used to transmit massages in security applications the signs recalls the physics status of the fibre optic when configured in a security sensor.

While fibre optic has been in use in telecommunications for several years, their deployment for security poses to yet to take off in this country. That they are highly cost effective in the long run has been applied proved through actual use abroad. Not only do they reduce man power but have the added advantage of being used in conjunction with available system of surveillance to achieve enhanced and more reliable security. Collaboration with manufactures abroad for fabricating such systems here is perhaps the need of the hour.

Motivating for Result

Katherin Xin

In tough times, money is scarce, and motivation becomes even more critical. In this session, right during the session, we will show you how to improve motivation in two ways at no cost beyond that you already incurred to come to this symposium. Can you improve your situation without extra spending? Yes, and we will prove it to you in this "hands on" session.

Every manger can benefit from an increased understanding of motivation. Managers responsible for safety have an even greater advantage from understanding motivation, which we will explain in some detail. Basically, you want to increase your ability to set up an environment of motivation in your organization for two quite different reasons.

First, safety managers, as with every practicing manager, wants to have as productive an organization as possible, public officials and managers alike want the nations, your nations, many nations to be as productive as possible. The better we can deal with this topic, the better off will be our workers, our organizations, our society. With this in mind, in section one of this report, we will review some classic ideas about motivation, and we will show how they can apply to you today.

Second, as managers in the safety arena, we have special needs. One of those needs is to insure that those at the top of the ladder know about dangerous situations or practices at the bottom. You need to know about things that may be happening which may lead to hazard, or even to disaster. But, in some organizations, the climate is such that no one wants to tell the boss that company safety policies are not being followed. People fear that the person who reports a problem or potential problem may come under attack. Perhaps this is not a new or isolated problem: we remember the ancient Roman leader who gave the order to "slay the bearer of bad tidings. " Are there dangers hidden in your organization that you do not even know about? In some cases, does "everyone else" know about these but does social pressure, or the unwritten policies of intermediate supervisors, prevent this information from getting to you? In section two of this report, we will show you how to assess your organizational climate on this dimension, and we will actually help you conduct a preliminary test of that climate.

I. Motivation for Productivity

In the past, the major forms of "motivation" took the form, of fear of punishment – physical, financial and social. But today, many theories of motivation exist that managers can use to improve their understanding of why people behave as they do. None provides a universally accepted explanation of human behavior. People are far too complex. There are many theories of motivation. I will discuss some of what we know about motivation from two perspectives : Content theories and process theories.

Content theories: Content theories of motivation are concerned with identifying what it is within an individual or the work environment that energize and sustain behavior. Simply, what specific things motivate people? On the other hand, process theories try to explain and describe the process of how behavior is energized, directed, and finally stopped.

Process theories: Process theories try to answer three questions: (1). Should I work hard? (2) How hard do I need to work? (3) How long do I have to keep this pace?

In the following paragraphs, I will first discuss two content theories: Maslow's need hierarchy and Herzberg's two-factor theory. Second, two process theories, Vroom's expectancy theory and Skinner's reinforcement theory, will be reviewed.

Maslow's Hierarchy of Needs Theory

There are many theories of motivation. One of my favorites has little or no statistical validity, little or no scientific basis, yet seems to help practicing managers understand their employees better. This is the theory of Abraham Maslow, who wrote his ideas over fifty years ago. Maslow's need hierarchy theory has enjoyed widespread acceptance since it was introduced. He identified 20 needs, which are hypothesized into five levels of needs.

Basically, Maslow held that individuals are driven by different kinds of needs at different times and in different circumstances, depending on the situation. He divided needs into a hierarchy of needs. (1) First, physiological needs drive behavior. (2) Second, safety and security needs. He was probably not aware of the India Institute of Safety and Security Management when he wrote, but he did group these two together, and said they were the MOST important needs, after the survival needs such as food and water in the physiological needs category. (3) Third, social needs also motivate. (4) Fourth, Maslow held that people are motivated by a need for self esteem, or ego satisfaction. (5) Fifth and last, we are motivated by the desire for self actualization.

There are some important aspects to Maslow's theory. For one thing, he suggested that typically humans would be driven to satisfy these groups of needs in order. When an individual has nothing, the physiological needs will dominate. The first priority of a person without food is to get food. Physiological needs are the driving force at that time. However, once a person has food, new and higher needs come to drive behavior. That is when the human being starts to focus on safety and security needs, according to Maslow. A key aspect of this description is that once a group of needs are somewhat satisfied, the next class of needs seems to dominate. For example, if a person has physiological needs met, and also has met safety and security needs, then social needs will tend to drive behavior. If this group of needs are basically satisfied, with the person content with his or her group of friends, then ego or self satisfaction needs tend to take center stage. Although neither social or ego needs can never be fully satiated, when these needs are basically taken care of, the need for self actualization comes into play. Maslow had a tough time defining self actualization, and I cannot really do better than the author of the idea. But, to me, self actualization is doing the thing you always wanted to accomplish, for no reason other than to prove to yourself that you can. The person who climbs a Himalayan mountain peak must be driven by the need of self actualization.

There is an important aspect of Maslow's theory that has to be mentioned here. A satisfied need is not a motivator. Once a person has enough food, food will not motivate. Further, safety and security are critical, but once satisfied, these areas will not MOTIVATE. However, the areas of social, ego or self esteem, and even more so, self actualization, can never be fully satisfied. The implications for management are significant. Social, ego and self actualization can always motivate. And, if you think about it, you can help your employees reach social goals, and ego goals, without cost to your organization. To the extent you allow people to choose their own work groups, they may be able to meet social goals. Of course, you do not want to sponsor a permanent party or celebration, but when we discuss the next theory, you will see that the team will feel more motivated if they are accomplishing.

Herzberg's Two Factor Theory

Another theory that practicing managers find worth studying is that of Frederick Herzberg, developed from studies conducted in

1959. He based his theory on a study of need satisfaction and on the reported motivational effects of these satisfaction on 200 engineers and accountants. The theory is referred to as the two factor theory of motivation. Based on the study, he reached two conclusions: (1). Some conditions of a job operate primarily to dissatisfy employees when they are not present. However the presence of these conditions does not build strong motivation. Herzberg called these maintenance factors. (2) Some job conditions build high levels of motivation and job satisfaction. However, if these conditions are not present they do not prove highly dissatisfying. He described six of these motivational factors.

A key point here is that the factors in one group are not the same as the factors in the other group. Hence, the "two factor theory." The distinction between motivational and maintenance factors is similar to what psychologists have describe as intrinsic and extrinsic motivators. External factors, called hygiene of maintenance factors, can be manipulated only to eliminate dissatisfaction. To motivate people, organizations need to address motivational factors. And, the lucky thing is, the motivating factors typically cost you, the manager nothing, we will demonstrate this conclusively.

During this conference we will prove to you that the basic ideas of this Herzberg theory, and the Maslow theory which preceded it, are sound. They can help you motivate, without spending extra money, which is always an important factor in tough times.

These content theories, even though quite old, are still referred to by thousands of practicing managers. They were not really developed scientifically, but they have a 'common sense' appeal. They can help you as well.

Process Theories

In contrast to the two content theorists, Maslow's need hierarchy and Herzberg's two factors, expectancy theory and reinforcement theory are process theories. They concentrate on how motivation occurs, is directed, sustained and stopped.

The expectancy theory of motivation as initially presented in 1964 by psychologist Victor Vroom views motivation as a process governing choices. He suggests that individuals are motivated at work to make different choices, such as the decision to participate, and decision to participate at a certain level. The logic of expectancy motivation is that individuals will exert work effort to achieve performance that will result in preferred rewards. The key concepts of Vroom's expectancy theory are valence, instrumentality and expectancy. Sometimes people call it the VIE model. This model will be demonstrated in the seminar.

Reinforcement theory is another widely discussed process theory of motivation, based largely on the work of psychologist B.F. Skinner. Reinforcement theory considers the use of positive and negative reinforces to motivate or create an environment to motivate. This theory of motivation is not concerned with needs or why people make choices. Instead it focuses on the environment and its consequences for the person.

Reviewing all the motivational theories discussed above, they all contain the theme that motivation is goal directed, although the theories use different terms and appear to be quite different they are not completely in conflict with each other. Basically they look at some segment of overall motivation or look at the same aspect of motivation from a slightly different perspective. Professor Lyman Porter and Edward Lawler offer an integrating mode of motivation based on all the theories discussed above.

The Porter-Lawler model points out the relationship or performance, satisfaction, and rewards and introduces the importance of having individuals performing jobs for which they have the proper skills, abilities and traits. There is also an issue of performance measurement. Performance must be measured accurately and systematically so that rewards can be distributed equitably. If no meaningful difference in rewards is made between high and low performance, high performers will lose motivational intensity and probably cut back on their performance.

In sum, motivation theories discuss what motivates people at an individual and organizational level. Of course, we are living in a global era. People from different cultures may have different needs and expectations. Organizations from different culture might employ different motivational strategies. But in every culture, certain basic ideas prevail. You can use these ideas to help your organization improve productivity.

At the same time, it is important not to overstate the importance of motivation. It takes more than motivation to accomplish organizational, or personal, goals. Edgar Schein puts it simply.

Schein reminded us that, the ability of the person, the nature of the work setting, the tools and materials available to do the job, the nature of the job itself, and the ability of management to coordinate employee, group, and departmental efforts – all enter into organizational effectiveness. So, when you apply the ideas discussed here, remember that there are other things in the equation also, such as the state of your equipment.

II. Motivation for an Open Environment

In addition to studying motivation for enhanced productivity, safety and security managers need to be concerned about motivation of a very different kind. If you do not know policies are being violated, your organization many run into serious problems. A survey of some recent maritime accidents in the USA reveals some interesting points.

In reach of four recent accidents, accident summaries reviewed one common denominator, crew or human error. In each accident, failures in upward communication flow had a bearing on the results.

Accident #1: The ramming of the U.S. fishing vessel Chickadee by the guided-missile frigate USS Richard L. Page in the Atlantic Ocean Virginia Beach, Virginia on April 21, 1987. The page officer on deck (OOD) failed to treat reported radar contact as a vessel in part because of fatigue and stress. The OOD did not have confidence in the ability of the radar operator and thus did not acknowledge the operator's reports. The OOD failed to communicate his concerns to the Commanding officer (CO) about the authenticity of the radar reports. The lack of information flow upwards was one casual factor in this accident.

Accident #2: The ramming of the Sidney Lanier Bridge by the Polish bulk carrier Ziemia Bialostocka at Burnswick, Georgia, on May 3, 1987. The pilot of the Zieam Bialostocka misjudged the turning capability of the vessel because he did not make himself aware of and use all available information. The pilot did not have knowledge of the technical parameters that affected the maneuvering characteristics of a vessel, information which was known to others on the ship. The lack of information flow upwards was one causal factor in this accident.

Accident #3: The ramming of the Spanish bulk carrier Urduliz by the aircraft carrier USS Dwight D. Eisenhower at Hampton Roads, Virginia on August 29, 1988. The probable cause of the accident was the delayed and insufficient action to correct the Eisenhower's deviation from the intended track by the navigator and the OOD because of inexperience in piloting the vessel through the resurrected channel in Hampton Roads. The OOD was overly concerned with arriving precisely on time at the harbor and slowed down the vessel in order to "look professional," In addition, a pilot was not utilized in this case. Most naval vessels do not utilize the services of pilots, at least in part, because they believe that the use of the pilot implies that the crew does not measure up to the navigation task. Expert guidance was available, but not used. And finally, the CO's attention had been diverted from the vessel's navigation to other duties during a critical period (an Admiral came on board). All the above cultural norms functioned in such a way that they overshadowed the roper navigation of the vessel. In addition, lack of information flow from those who know the channel to those making navigational decisions, was one casual factor in this accident.

Accident #4: The ramming of the French tank ship Camargue, by the Swedish auto carrier Figaro in the Gulf of Mexico Galveston, Texas on November 10, 1988. The probable cause of the collision was the

Figaro pilot's determination to overtake the tank ship in the entrance channels to GALVESTON Bay and the master's and pilot's lack of action to abort the overtaking. The pilot of the Figaro and the pilot of the Camargue did not exchange information regarding the speed of their vessels. Once again, there was a general lack of communication and overconfidence on the part of the pilot. If all concerned reported what they knew, this accident could have been prevented.

These little case stories are from one small area, naval ramming. However, information from a wide variety of settings leads to painfully similar conclusions: too often those who need critical information do not receive it. And, more times than we would like, incidents occur, incidents which can be in part attributed to the lack of upward communication of ideas and facts. Frequently, the information is withheld in spite of policies that "bad news should be transmitted upwards," but this does not take place, why?

Recent findings show that one key factor is the organizational climate. To achieve a safe organization, you need an open organization. There are several ways to improve oneness, which we will discuss at the seminar. First, however, we recommend each organization assess the climate to determine oneness. We will provide a sample survey form, the use of which we will demonstrate during the seminar.

Conclusions

Each of us is interested in motivation, especially in tough times. As managers responsible for safety and security, we have an even greater need to motivate employees. In our case, it may be a matter of life or death at times. Fortunately, social scientists have given us some tools to work with, and hopefully these will help us do our jobs better.

Crime Prevention Through Environmental Design

Randy Atlas

In the field of security litigation a new concern is emerging: Liability for crimes that occur in the parking lots and premises owned by restaurant. Lounges, Shopping malls, Apartments, Hotels, Grocery stores and other commercial establishments. Four reasons for this development can be cited. The first reason deals with changes in the law that allow individuals to sue for crimes committed at a place of business. Proprietors have always been responsible for providing adequate security for their patrons. In the past however, case law limited this responsibility for providing security to the physical structure in which business was conducted .

— **Michaeld Wiatrowski**

Therefore, if a restaurant had been robbed several times or was in a neighborhood where violent crime was a problem and where additional crimes might be foreseeable, then the proprietor was obligated to provide security for patrons while they were within the physical structure of the building.

In part, this interpretation of the law is understandable. Common sense would seem to dictate that crime committed outside a business would be the responsibility of the police department and not the proprietor. Criminals come from the community into a business's property and therefore should be interdicted by law enforcement officers rather than private security officers. In some instances, proprietors have asked municipal law enforcement agencies to patrol their propriety specifically their parking lots, but have been told that service is not a law enforcement function. In these cases, the failure of the proprietor and the security planner to accept the responsibility security themselves lays the foundation for lawsuits involving the failure to provide proper security.

In recent years however litigation has become more explicit in extending the responsibility of a proprietor to the promises propriety line rather than just to the doorway. This change means providing the same level of security on the grounds and in the parking lot as the level dictated by the nature of the security problem in the area in general.

The second reason for increase in security cases focuses on proprietors who are willing to arrange for adequate security both inside and outside their place of business, but who fail to use the services of professional security planners. Some proprietors may retain a security firm that makes recommendations about alarm systems and guard services without first completing a comprehensive security survey and preparing an overall security plan.

In their haste to sell guard services and hardware ,these security representatives may recommend developing only part of a total security system rather than one oriented toward the prevention of crime and the protection of clients. As a result, the system that is implemented may address only a narrow range of security concerns, such as robbery protection rather than providing for the security of patrons regardless of whether they are inside the building or on the proprietor's property.

The third reason deal with the failure of security professionals to be aware of the implication of case law as it pertains to security planning. It could be argued that a change in the legal environment as well as a change in the physical and social environment should trigger a reanalysis of the security plan. But in many instances, security planning has been one step behind case law. As a minimum, security planners should apprise proprietors of the implications of legal developments for security planning, particularly when increased levels of security are called for by statutory and case law. To date , the security profession is relatively theoretical and is therefore without models or examples that provide a framework for analysis. An environmental systems model, such as the one discussed in this article, provides such a framework for analysis. A fourth reason for increases in security litigation can be identified.

In some instances, recommendations made by security professionals are not adequate or are not implemented. For example, the established security plan for a sports facility was not implemented during a rainstorm because the officers on duty were more concerned with staying dry than with performing their patrols. Therefore, no one was in position to prevent as assault on a patron of the sports facility.

A model for analyzing relevant points for a wide range of security issues, called an Environmental Systems Model, is derived from research on general systems theory. The model examines the development of a security system through three phases, threat analysis, security system development, and evaluation.

Throughout this assessment, security is treated as a dynamic process rather than as a static entity. By using this model, security planners can respond to problems before they surface to become serious threats against life and property.

This model treats crime prevention as an ongoing process or system rather than as the mere application of checklists against a problem. It emphasizes an analysis of the crime problem or the threat, the development of a prevention system and the evaluation of the system to assess how effectively it is performing. To show how the three phases of the model are use. The various steps in the model will be applied to the specific problem of parking lot crime.

Phase one

Threat are the potential acts or conditions that may cause loss or harm to individual. For parking lots, a threat analysis begins by defining the nature of the crime problem in the neighborhood surrounding the facility. To acquire this information, the security planner may need to contact a local law enforcement agency and request a print-out of the types of crimes that occurred in the area during the past year. The analysis may show that crimes are occurring in adjacent areas as well as the premises itself or that such crimes are becoming more frequent or more serious. In this case, it can be assumed that a crime occurring in the area could be defined as foreseeable in a court of law.

The ongoing analysis of neighborhood crimes is, therefore a valuable piece of information. Anecdotal information is also important, of crimes that are reported to the police, the reputation of an area can provide information that can dictate whether security should be increased. A court may direct that it is reasonable to a proprietor should have known a threat existed if everyone else in the neighborhood agreed crime was a serious problem. Finally, incidents reported by patrons or security officers can provide the security planner with information in the nature of the current problem.

At one grocery store, for example, the parking lot had attracted a number of panhandlers who would snatch customer's groceries, walk them to the car, and then demand money for the assistance. One of these panhandlers later assaulted and killed an individual who was passing through the parking lot. These incidents had been reported by both the patrons and the security guards but were not considered by the corporate security planners. A lawsuit followed the assault, which was deemed to have been foreseeable, and a settlement resulted.

Professional literature is also an important source of material in conducting threat and crime analysis. Industry journals frequently provide forums where problems are presented and approaches to solving the problems are discussed. For example, hospital journals have documented the increased vulnerability of hospitals to both internal as well as external losses. Periodicals on restaurant and lounge management describe the problems caused by altercations on the premises resulting from serving alcohol to intoxicated individuals. While an individual facility may not have experienced a certain problem, these publications apprise the security planner of security concerns recognized in the industry for which counter measures should be developed.

Phase Two

Security System Development. The development of specific recommendations for the security of a parking lot should be based on the threat assessment completed in Phase One. This information should then be added to an assessment of the environment of the facility needing protection and the nature of the business conducted there. With this information, the security planner can then consider developing specific physical security measures along with security personnel requirements. Finally, contingency plans can be developed and an evaluation system can be set in place.

Environment Assessment: The environment of the parking lot and its relationship to such factors as streets, stores, houses and schools must be considered before developing any security plan. The physical design of the parking lot can help to determine if the facility is a thoroughfare for pedestrians who might be potential criminals, or if it is a meeting place where illegal transactions could occur. The design of the parking lot can limit entry and allay the perception that the lot can be used for purposes other than the intended ones.

The design and location of entrances and exits can also help to control individuals who may be cruising the lot looking for routes that are controlled. A criminal may look elsewhere. Similarly, design factors such as low shrubs can separate public areas from private parking lots that may only be used by persons with legitimate reasons for being there. Thus individuals seen crossing over the shrubs into these areas can be identified as intruders.

Facility Assessment

The nature of the facility itself is an, important element in the threat analysis. A parking lot for a bank or a casino presents a different type of setting than a parking lot for a clothing store. In one case, the security for a gambling facility was concentrated in the lobby. An individual who had won a large amount of money did not know the casino would provide a security escort to the parking lot. As a result the patron entered the parking lot alone and was robbed. Similarly, security planners responsible for protecting the parking lots of bars and other establishments where liquor is served should be attentive to the potential problems that could be caused by intoxicated patrons. If customers become disruptive, they should be escorted from the premises rather than simply taken to the door. The parking lots of certain types of establishments can become sites for illegal activities or fight. While the proprietor may not be aware of these problems, a court may state that it was the responsibility of the owner to keep the property under surveillance and to become familiar with be activities occurring on the premises thus establishing the proprietor's reliability for failing to maintain control. Access control fencing is an appropriate method of controlling access to parking lots. Depending upon the level of the threat, the type of fencing used at any one location can range from decorative fencing, which simply demarcate the parking lot from the street, to security fencing which serves to control access. If fencing is needed both for access control a property, delineation the security planner should recommend a higher level of fencing than the circumstances may seem to dictate. For example, if the choice is between a six-foot decorative fence or a six-foot security fence, six-foot security fence should be chosen even though the decorative fence may seem to be adequate.

Lighting

Lighting as an element of an overall security plan for parking lots has traditionally reserved a great deal of attention. Obviously, lights in a parking lot are placed so they illuminate areas where criminals may hide. While the type of illumination is relatively unimportant the level of illumination is a critical factor.

The Illuminating Engineering Society (IES) of North America has established Illumination Standards For Parking Lots. IES recommends that self-parking areas be illuminated at a level of I lux and that valet parking areas have a 2.2 lux level of illumination. These levels are being recognized as the standards against which the adequacy of illumination is being judged in the courts. The failure to meet those standards therefore be comes a factor in establishing the liability of the proprietor.

Present Day Challenges to Security

Joginder Singh

Security is the basic need of not only for the human beings but also for the industry as well. Each industry wants to protect itself not only from its competitors, but also from other elements that would intrude upon it and damage it. One of the type of providing physical security is protection of the perimeters according to the man and the machine inside the premises. . The necessity of physical security is being revised not only by the industry but also by almost every individual and every organization including the government offices. The presence of physical security would naturally deter unauthorized persons to gain access to the persons or the industry to be protected. Deterrence can be achieved not only by the physical presence of the human beings but also by sealed doors and by sophisticated items like automatic access control and closed circuit TV etc. Many times the physical security overlaps and joins with the sophisticated security, which is comparatively very expensive, but any security system cannot be all-exclusive.

Implementation of the physical security varies again with the type of industry and the type of persons employed and the degree of physical security required. Basically security is not a welcome feature because it puts restraints. It is also a fact of life that no restraint of any kind is welcome. However in the events of threats and risks lot of emphasis is laid on the security. According to Mr. W. Reddaway, a Group services manager, who has worked in the united nations, the objective of industrial security is "Profit and productivity". In the case of an organization that is not in the commercial sector the objectives of security is organizations success and lowered cost.

Industrial security is concerned with asset protection and loss prevention within an organization. The assets referred to include the buildings, the material, the plant and machinery, the personnel, the information, the skills and knowledge and even the public goodwill and confidence in the organization. All of these assets are worthy of protection. Loss prevention encompasses losses caused by theft, by fraud, by vandalism, by fire, flood, wind etc. Security seeks to reduce or eliminate these losses within the context of an approach known as Risk management. This approach takes a very broad based look at the losses.

If the employees involved get more confident they will increase the amount they steal. When it gets discovered, you have the cost of an investigation into long serving staff, suspicions all through the plant and real risk of labour unrest. That may mean slower production. It may mean strike action. When cases go to court they may be thrown out on a technicality and you face claims of unfair dismissal. This will take up management time and cost lawyer's fees for years.

If it is reported in the media, it will give you bad publicity and cause doubts in customer's mind which will affect your reliability as a supplier. They may then give some contracts to your competitor as a precaution and your company suffers again. Your company will also suffer if good, potential employees decide that your company sounds less attractive to work for than your competitor and staff, concerned for the future, think about leaving. It goes on and on. Dozens of actions may happen each damaging your business.

The role of the Industrial Security personnel should be as under:

At Senior Level

1. Knowledge of the business of the organization, its position in the market; its competitors; its vulnerabilities; its opportunities and plans for the future.
2. A thorough understanding of processes within the physical premises of the organization and beyond.
3. Knowledge of its major and/or critical sources, performance, movement of raw materials, components, finished goods, terms of other items on this list.
4. Sources of control data on production performance, movement of raw materials, components, finished goods etc. and the knowledge to interpret them.
5. Knowledge of the site and of all hazards (security, fire and safety) within it or adjacent to it.
6. Thorough knowledge of the physical, electronic and manned responses available to meet risks as well as the potential for risk reduction or risk transfer.
7. Analytical ability to define problems and solutions and the financial knowledge required to present them as investment options and talk them through within senior management.

At a Middle Management Level

1. A thorough knowledge of the activities and processes within the site (s) for which he is responsible and of the transportation and distribution systems .
2. Complete awareness of all hazards (security, fire and safety) within his site (s) and adjacent to it.
3. Thorough knowledge of the physical, electronic measures in relation to ever-changing risks/hazards and to be able to implement or recommend changed security measures in the light of changed risks.

4. The ability to audit the existing security measures in relation to changing risks / hazards and to implement or recommend changed security measures in the light of changed risks.
5. Knowledge and ability to direct and/ or conduct investigations into incidents or alleged incidents in a manner appropriate to an internal investigation.
6. Experience in defusing, controlling or containing aggression expressed by individuals or groups from inside or outside the organization.
7. Management knowledge and ability to run a service department in a cost effective way including plan, budget, control cost, manage personnel etc.
8. Leadership ability and style appropriate to the security role and the ability to gain trust and support from all employees.
9. Knowledge of emergency service and public order organizations with which he will have to liaise.

At a Junior Level

1. Sufficient knowledge of the activities of the site, at which they work to enable them, to identify unusual or abnormal events or behavior.
2. Thorough knowledge of procedures etc. that they must carry out.
3. Trained observation skills and ability to be vigilant.
4. Thorough knowledge of procedure, documentation, materials etc. which they must check.
5. Security fire and safety knowledge sufficient to enable them to identify risks that may be encountered in their daily routine.
6. Ability to make a simple report on an incident or risk either verbally or preferably in writing.
7. Good interpersonal skills for both routine and more difficult situations.
8. Strong motivation and commitment to the provision of a service that protects the site, promote good relations within the

organizations and enhance the organization's image externally. The range of knowledge and ability described for each of these levels is considerable and it is unlikely that any person transferring into a security role at any level will ever have all of it. There is one attribute which is referred to as a service function which is to manage and operate, a range of "clients" both inside and outside the organization.

Industrial development is the backbone of the economy, but at the same time the economy cannot be developed if it is exposed to various hazards. Depending upon the degree of sophistication required for industrial security, gadgetries like infrared, senses, night vision devices, fire detectors, sensors can be used. However, this will again depend upon several factors like physical structure of the land building and type of equipment, the stores, personal know how, trade secrets, labour problems and above all the financial resources the organization is willing to spend for the security management, i.e. for prevention, detection and intervention.

The Human Aspect of Security and Safety

Saru S Rangnekar

Every industrial function has three dimensions:

- Technology System
- Human Aspect

Technology & System

Technology is the hardware used to carry out the function. In this generation, there has been an explosive growth in the technological innovations available for all industrial functions–including security and safety. The technology available in manufacturing processes have made a revolutionary change in the quality and productivity in those functions.

System evolved to support the technology have also become sophisticated and have helped the quality and productivity e.g. through TQM (Total quality Management).

However, in security and safety (as in all service industries), the productivity is still a serious problem in spite of systems studies and investment of capital in technology. Following are the problem areas:

- In manufacturing industry, capital can replace labor (e.g. robots replacing production workers). In security and safety, capital can only provide tools to the workers–whether those tools would help productivity or harm it depends on what the workers do with them.
- In manufacturing industry, working "smarter" (i.e. finding how best to do the task) improved productivity. In security and safety productivity can be increased only if the worker knows what the task is and why it is to be performed.
- In manufacturing industry, the work is organized to facilitate concentration. In security and safety, splintered attention is the norm. This automatically reduces the productivity of time.
- Sometimes the basic objective of the job is forgotten to attend to the auxiliary tasks–like security man spending his time filling forms rather than in attending to security.

Meeting the challenge

The first step to meet the challenge of productivity in security and safety is to define the task, concentrate work on the task and define performance in quality and quantity. This will ensure that the effective tasks will be performed to give efficient service. The second step is to ask the workers to address themselves to both productivity and quality. Traditionally, security workers are regarded as dumb, immature or maladjusted. However, most of them have a good idea about the work they are doing–its logic and rhythm, its quality and tools. This knowledge the workers have about their job is the starting point for improving productivity, quality and performance. In security and safety, partnership with responsible worker is the only way to improve productivity.

Continuous learning must accompany productivity gains. The greatest benefit of training comes not from learning something new–but from doing better what we already do well.

In security and safety, workers learn most when they teach. The best way to improve a star performer's productivity is to ask him to present "the secret of my success" before his peers. Every security and safety unit has to become learning institution.

Human Aspect: The key factor

Fortunately, we are in a position to raise the productivity in security and safety. We can define the tasks, concentrate work on the task by minimizing splintering of attention and define performance in quality and quantity. We can also make the employees as partners in productivity improvement and be the first source of ideas for it, put teaching as part of the job of every security and safety worker. This will not only increase the productivity but also increase the workers' self- respect and pride.

To raise the productivity of service work, we cannot rely on government or politicians. It is the task of managers in the security and safety functions–it is the prime social responsibility of management in the society of the future.

Limitations & Hurdles in Prevention of Crimes

S M Wadekar

Objective of setting up of any industry is to produce more and be prosperous. In order to achieve such objectives, many disciplines are gathered for skilled operations.

"Security" is one of the many functions which fulfill a company's objectives.

In the performance of security duties, i.e. protecting company's property against theft, fire, pilferage, apprehending thieves and trespassers into the premises of works, searching them and producing them before police and lodging complaints on a part of their day to day work. Therefore, a security officer is mainly responsible for the protection of property.

Sections 96 to 106 of Indian Penal Code dealing with the right of private defence are important provisions of law, having a vital bearing on the day to day activities of every individual. These sections define the nature, scope and extent of limitations of certain acts which under normal circumstances would be punishable as offences. But sometimes are made justifiable and not treated as offences, if committed for the purpose of protecting the person or property either of one's own or of any other person and that is how a security officer tries to protect property against crime.

The security personnel of a private industrial concern do not have any special powers or privileges as the police have for the performance of their duties. The law, however has bestowed certain limited rights and privileges on all citizens and they provide the necessary legal sanction for the different activities of the security personnel in the performance of their duty. Encountering, chasing and capturing a gang of thieves committing theft of company's property or opposing and removing encroachment on company's land etc, and they have no choice other than exercising the right of private defence.

Security attempts to provide protections against all forms of losses stemming from artificial natural or environmental hazards, therefore, the built–in security which is very important aspect has been ignored in our country. The term security i.e. protection against any threat within is used in many different contexts, such as national security, international security, internal security, retail security, physical security, industrial security and information security. All of these aspects can be involved in building security depending on the use of occupancy of the building and nature of work. I am not aware of such building code converging built in security aspect in our country and if available, it is not being implemented.

Power of Security

Industrial security personal have to face many problems which are being faced by the police officers during the course of their duties.

Security department is supposed to be the first line of industrial defense, in that the numbers of offences committed are reported against property and human body. As stated in the chapters 4 to 30 of the Indian Penal Code, industrial securities personnel are also confronted with the following offences while performing their duty;

- Sections 121 to 126 both inclusive, and Section 130 (that is to say offences against the state specified in Chapter VI of the said code).

- Section 143, 144, 145, 147 and 148 (that is to say, offence against the public tranquility specified in Chapter VIII of the said code).
- Sections 161 to 165-A both inclusive (that is to say, offences relating to illegal gratification)
- Sections 272 to 278, both inclusive (that is to say, offences relating to adulteration of food and drugs, etc)
- Section 302, 306 and 304 (that is to say, offense affecting life)
- Section 382 (that is to say, offence of theft after preparation made for cussing death hurt or restraint in order to the committing of the theft)
- Section 392 to 399, both inclusive and Section 402 (that is to say, offences of robbery and dacoity)
- Section 409 (that is to say offence relating to criminal breach of trust by public servant etc)
- Section 431 to 439, both inclusive (that is to say, offences of mischief against property)
- Section 449 and 450 (that is to say offence of house trespass)
- Section 489-A to 489-E both inclusive (that is to say offence restating to currency notes and bank notes)

In the absence of any reasonable excuse, the burden of proving which excuse shall like upon the person aware, forth with information is to be given to nearest magistrate or police officer or commissioner.

Many Hurdles

Increasing unemployment, socio-economic problems, general deterioration in law and order situation and ever increasing terrorism and violence are also confronting the industries. Time lost for reporting of such crimes, invites repetition of attempts by criminals.

Almost all big industries work in 3 shifts, i. e. 24 hours and crime can take - place at any hour of duty. The following facts have been experienced by security department for abnormal delay in reporting crime to police station due to various circumstances.

- Location of police station, *chowky* or outpost for factory under jurisdiction,
- Absence of facility for direct communication,
- Time for police officer to report on scene,
- Registration of FIR,
- Time for *panchanama* and recording evidence and statement,
- Investigation and final report

Offence in industries are normally repeated from the following IPC sections:-

382, 392, to 399, 409, 431, to 439, 449

When a case is detected by security, all formalities should be completed without wasting time.

- Criminal disappear with the stolen property,
- Property is sold out to third party; &
- Criminals flee away.

Moreover, once the case is registered with the police there is no association of the security officer with the investigation, even though he know details of a case better than a police officer. This causes:

- Further delay for lodging complaint.
- Security staff to report police station with crime and property.
- Decision for lodging's a complaint by police.
- Visitation of police officer and *panchanama* formalities.

It is also experienced that police officers are generally reluctant to register cases of crimes or posted from the industries as they do not consider them serious crimes.

Further hurdles are the police having lack of investigation skills, their hesitation to attach property, non disclosure of stolen property receivers, delay in conducting raids to apprehend criminals and lower assessment of gravity of crime.

Suspecting security staff for connivance, use of derogatory language, non-availability of police staff at police station, from mobility of force, i.e. absence of vehicles, protracted investigations and frequent change of investigating officers.

- Reluctance in disclosing the progress of case to security staff.

- Pressure tactics and re-recording of statement for failure of any case.
- Abnormal delay in the trial of cases, grant of bail, casual approach for prosecution.

From the above narration, it is concluded that despite having power with police, the police department takes casual approach for the offences reported from the industries and thereby there are many attempts by the criminals and the security department becomes helpless in preventing crimes in industries.

In the absence of sufficient powers other than right of private defense, the result and the success of such cases are very limited. A criminal apprehended needs to be interrogated, detained, arresting other accomplice, and recovery of the stolen property which is beyond the power of security officer and considering the major crimes and law and order problem police officer cannot extend assistance with this reasonable time.

It has been past experience that crimes committed in industries are repeated since the punishment is not awarded in a reasonable time limit. Once the powers are given to security officer, it will motivate them to control crime.

Job satisfaction always demand wants to be satisfied. In absence, this upsets the morals of any security department.

Suggestions

Police and security liaison:

- Formation of security cell in the vicinity of police inspectors jurisdiction.
- Suitable training for security staff for assisting police for maintenance of law and order as well crime prevention duties.
- Appointment of qualified fire officers for investigating of fire cases under section 435 IPC.
- Mutual aid scheme amongst security organizations for all types of emergencies and information on crimes and criminals.
- Issue of identity cards to security personnel for prevention of

crime and apprehension of criminal with limited power.

- Wireless / telephone communication to important industries for active assistance for prevention of crime and call for assistance.

This paper is being concluded with the request to high police officials and delegates present in the seminar to formulate codes and procedures for powers to assist security organizations for prevention of crimes and losses in industries. While concluding this paper, I would like to quote an expert's opinion on the subject.

> "Perhaps we will find security officers appointed locally, in the American way, who actually patrol villages and towns and if there is something really serious, a policeman will be sent for to take the people away. Perhaps we will find security officers being granted powers of arrest having received a certain amount of training, to detain people for crimes of, what we used to call in the old days, petty larceny and damage, and take them before the justice, the following day. In cases of major crimes, murders, serious accidents, all kinds of arson attacks, sexual attacks etc, the local CID would be brought in."

— COL, Sabastian Moran

Striking The Wrong Note With One-man Bands*

The end of yet another year sees the security industry apparently very healthy and expanding at a great rate, with a proliferation of security companies springing up all over the country.

There is, at present, no legislation, no checking, no vetting or barring on any of the one-end two – man bands who go out and see security. And yet, when you think about it, one wonderful industry does not get into too much trouble compared with many other groups of people in the public eye.

---

* Extract from Security and Protection Equipment December 1989. By Col Sebastian Moran

So I, as an old man, congratulate all the members of the security industry for a good year of honest toil and industry and for supporting the forces of law and order in their time of tribulation.

Sub-Human

Let us think of some of the things that have happened. We had the sub – human creatures that put a bomb on a plane flying over Scotland. Are their masters happy with the year they have had? The Republican army, amongst others, kneecapping people, using Black & Decker drills on people to extract confessions and shooting innocent young children. Do they consider it has been a good year? What about the new crime now, which is so popular, of attempting to extort money from large companies by threatening adulteration of their food products? "Perhaps in ten year's time we will find security officers appointed locally, In the American way, who actually patrol villages and towns."

What type of a world are we going to live in? What type of a world are my children going to live in? Is it never again going to be the kind of world I grew up in and spent my middle years in? Yes, I lived through two world wars, but how different things were, for how safe it was for women and children to walk the streets of our country between the wars. It was so safe in some areas that doors were left open or with a piece of string behind the door attached to the key, which could be pulled through the letter box to open the door.

Cars, that were tremendous status symbols, were left unlocked. Yes, there was the odd thief known to us, old time coppers who knew where they lived and where they worked. We even knew every vehicle on the road when we patrolled at night. We knew where people lived and what they were up to. But, seemingly, not now even if the number of security guards has probably risen by 25 percent this year.

Disarray

Much fuss and play has been made about the police, we are our first line of defence from the lawless, being seemingly in a state of total disarray. Demoralized, frightened to move into certain areas, afraid to move to other quarters. Sometimes inviting representatives from the press television and paparazzi to view drug raids and then they are surprised when they find there are no drugs. What on earth is going on ?

This is the year that has been the police statistics, in some areas totally untrue, inflated for their own best reasons. What on earth is going on? But now we have this baying for police blood and I think what we are actually doing, if we did but know it, is turning off the forces and order in our country.

If you want to see evidence of this, I would suggest you look at the increase in the number of Rottweiler dogs purchased, the increased number of burglar alarms installed; go into Don Caster or Parsley and wander past the houses there and you will see that virtually every house has a burglar alarm. Look at people now ushering and learning how to use shotguns.

Uninitiated

Look at the increased number of security guards throughout the United Kingdom. If anyone has bothered to keep the facts on the numbers of security guards, they would probably find it has gone up by 25 per cent this year. More and more companies are going back to the times before 1829. The river police followed the examples of our railways, when the railways hired their own security people.. Large companies are getting their own security managers and some even dress them to look like policemen and train them in the same way.

So, the picture that I paint and reflect on, whilst sitting in front of the fire, is one of an expanding industry, filling the space left by the retreating forces of law and order.

Where, I wonder will this all lead to in ten years time? Well, I doubt that I will still be here then but what will it mean for my children and their children in ten years? Possibly someone will have been given a kinghood for a blinding glimpse of the obvious which is if you put more light into an area, crime goes down. This also means that crime goes up in other areas that are not so well lit but it is a good theory, isn't it.

Patrol

Perhaps we will find security officers appointed locally, in the American way, who actually patrol villages and towns and if there is something really serious, a policeman will be sent for to take the people away. Perhaps we will find security officers being granted powers of arrest, having received a certain amount of training, to detain people for crimes of, what we used to call in the old days, petty larceny and damage, and take them before the justices the following day. In cases of major crimes, murders serious accidents, all kinds, of arson attacks, sexual attacks etc. the local CID would be brought in.

"I congratulate all the members of the security industry for a good year of honest toll and industry and for supporting the forces of law and order in their time of tribulation."

Motivating Employees of the Future

Renu Mattoo

The workplace of the future will fundamentally and permanently alter the relationship between managers and workers. These traditional adversaries will become partners. Managerial control will give way to employee self control. Authoritative, Directive and Controlling management will die out. No longer will managers seek quality performance from workers through forced obedience. Instead, managers of the future will seek to empower employees to rights and responsibilities of partnership with regards to products and the services they produce. They will perform their own inspections, identify defects and causes of poor quality, and make adjustments that they deem necessary. They will monitor their relations with customers needs, most of which they will anticipate in advance, and be able to rapidly create products and services to meet these needs. Most importantly, worker partners will be flexible willing to take on any assignment or perform any tasks necessary to help their company succeed. They will do what needs to be done when and where it needs to be done. They will adapt to and learn to love change.

Worker – partners will willingly do all of these things because of the way they will be motivated.

The workplace of the future will require that employees take initiative. Respond rapidly to changing circumstances and saturations, and be mentally alert and focused on the current organizational imperative. Rigid hierarchies will be dismantled, as will the ceremonial trappings of power. The goal will be to attach people mentally and emotionally to the workplace.

The difference between the traditional, control – oriented, scientifically managed workplace and the commitment oriented workplace of tomorrow are multi faceted.

The traditional workplace emphasizes individual responsibility for individual performance; has fixed jobs and job – contents; causes coordination and control to flow from top to down: legitimizes status and position; makes adversaries of workers and managers.

In tomorrow's workplace, emphasis will be on shared responsibility for group performance; jobs will be fluid and flexibility will be of paramount importance. Control will be shared and coordination will flow from shared goals and values; workers and managers will be partners.

Motivation will be of prime importance because the human resource will become something much more than an asset to be merely counted, tabulated, used, move and expended. More importantly, the human contribution will become more critical for success because the production and delivery system of the future will be chaotic, unpredictable and even perhaps, irrational. Over domination and control by managerial elite will become ineffective.

The importance of people rather than technology, as the key importance for success in the workplace of the future is well illustrated by the themes of some of America's most prominent future oriented companies;

Apple computer's Mike Campi says: "… the best way to keep great people is to allow them to feel like they make a difference."

What makes Apple a good place to work is the company's commitment to empowering people at all levels. Campi explains, "It's not the traditional supervisor telling the line operations people what to do it's really the line operations people working with the supervisor to make sure that all obstacles that might block their objectives are removed. That means giving them the right tools, working with them. This is what we mean by really giving people responsibility and empowering them with the authority to meet their objectives."

Form the CEO on down, the company is very frank about its business directions and new product strategies. While that candor may sometimes result in the competitions learning a bit too much, it also shows Apple's employees that the company is willing to share important information with them, showing them another sign of their power and value.

Digital's Bill Hanson says: "At Digital we feel very strongly that people will do the right thing... when they're given a sense of vision or a sense of direction, have access to information, are given responsibility. We trust the individual. In Digital's future, employees will look less like employees and more like employers and more like Partners in the business. As the employee employer relationship becomes similar to that of customer supplier, with well-defined and obvious benefits and independence for each party."

Thus, a company trust in employees, an open corporate culture, and an energetic, future oriented work environment make Digital a great place to work.

Hewlett Packard's Harold Motions says: "The heart of the thing is treating people as individuals, and trying as hard as you can to satisfy their needs."

The result is an atmosphere where employees are challenged, are urged and expected to be creative, to think individually, to take risks. "We try to make our engineers feel the sky is the limit," Edmondson says. "We give them a substantial amount of technical and intellectual freedom to do the right things."

We try to create an atmosphere in which employees can enjoy themselves and prosper and make significant contributions. We also try to be up front about what their future is likely to be, not only in terms of financial rewards. We all share a genuine desire for the individual to lead a full and rewarding life.

What instructions then can we give to mangers on the "new styles of motivating people?"

1. **Make people feel like champions the way Apple computer does.** Create an environment where he or she can make a difference. Make every person feel personally significant.
2. **Give people a mission.** Make it not just any mission, but something truly special. Such as "changing the world". Make working at the company something much more than just an economic exchange.
3. **Empower people through involvement.** Make the role of managers and supervisors a "helping" and facilitating" role. Act on the premise that people want to achieve – that they want to help the company succeed. Instead of having of managers and supervisors try to control employee behavior, have them focus on removing obstacles to employee performance. Assume that people can and will do extraordinary thing if institutional barriers to performance are removed.
4. **Be frank and open about the company's business strategies and direction.** Make sure everyone understands what "we" as a company are trying to accomplish. Don't be concerned if a competitor finds out about a particular strategy. Above all else, Don't keep secrets. Make sure everyone knows everything.
5. **Trust people to do the right thing.** Assume that given enough of the right information and enough self control people will act in the best interest of the company and presumably in their own best interest.
6. **Create a unique culture and indoctrinate people from the start do that culture.** Don't let an informal social system just develop over time. Visualize what the company should be like, and share that vision. Make sure everyone knows how to behave consistently with that vision, and reward people who

do it. If someone doesn't act in concert with the vision, express your disappointment and encourage him or her to change or leave.

Such might be the prescriptions for motivation in the workplace of the future. But what do they mean for the individual worker? On the positive side, they mean that the workplace will be purposely orchestrated to have greater meaning and significance for each of us personally than ever before. Working will be more than an economic exchange. It will be a search for daily meaning as well as daily bread, for recognition as well as cash for astonishment rather than torpor; in short, for a sort of like rather than a Monday through Friday sort of dying. To that extent, the workplace will be much better. But being given "daily meaning" in the work one does, also carries a price.

The workplace of the future will demand more from every worker, more than ever before, it will also give more – meaning, responsibility, purpose, autonomy, self-control. Each employee will have to decide on the value of that exchange.

Anti Terrorsim by System Design

Richard P Grassic

Designing a security system which effectively respond to terrorist and other threats presents a formidable challenge to the security system design engineer. System success will be based on the effectiveness of individual components to counter threat elements and reduce vulnerabilities.

System design engineers must visualize security threats and risks. Anticipate the worst situation and ultimately weigh the cost of any countermeasure recommendation against the perceived benefit gained. Determination of cost effective protective measures and their integration is the result of a structured decision process which considers the individual and collective contribution of each assessor's protection strategy according to the complete system's requirements.

Role of The Security Designer

The designer strives to achieve a synergistic relationship among the various components and subsystems selected. Selection of appropriate equipment, procedures, manpower levels, facilities and information is accomplished on the basis of the most reliable and capable combinations to meet the known and expected capabilities of the threat.

However the designer is constrained by limited and possibly decreasing budgets. Soaring personnel and equipment costs and ever-increasing external and internal threats. This demand a comprehensive systems approach to countermeasures selection and integration which minimizes asset vulnerability, minimizes initial system cost and keeps subsequent costs under control.

In the final analysis, the designer selects and integrates protective measures from the following range of subsystem options.

- Facilities and architectural barriers designed to deter and delay an adversary.
- Physical security equipment designed to assist detection and assess intrusion attempts and unauthorized activities.
- Communications systems that collect, integrate, transmit, and display alarm and other data for operator response and control response forces.
- Security personnel to conduct day to day security program operations, manage system support and responded to no routine events.
- Security procedures that guide security operations and provide direction and control.

Countermeasures Selection

Experience has shown that the countermeasures selection and overall system integration process must be structured and front – loaded in order for the designer to arrive at a valid security concepts. The process is based on a thorough analysis of threats and the relative exposure of individual assets to these threats. Thus, the initial accomplishment of thorough requirements analysis is critical to developing an optimum system configuration and retaining the relative cost-effectiveness of various protective design strategies and countermeasure options.

Initially assets that need protection are identified. And their criticality to the facility and its function are determined. Next, the attractiveness of these assets of potential threats and the likely modes of attack are evaluated. Finally areas in which existing countermeasures do not adequately address the threat are identified as facility vulnerabilities.

In order to be applied effectively countermeasures must be selected for each asset in terms of an applicable design basis threat(s). Likely modes of attack in terms of the potential use of tools, weapons and possibly explosives to be used at specific severity levels is also considered. A critical assumption of the process is an asset of highest critically to the user, coupled with its high attractiveness to an aggressor, will prompt a likely and probable aggressor to employ more force in an attack on that asset.

Likelihood of attack is expressed for each asset and potential aggressor(s) either high, medium, low or very low, this forces the designer to determine what is to be protected, its value to the user and aggressor alike, and its attractiveness to various aggressor types. This is usually expressed in terms of design basis threat parameters for each asset.

For security upgrade projects, countermeasures identification and selection can only occur after the designer has determined existing measures in place that can effectively be integrated into the system solution to deter, delay, deny, detect, assess and respond to attacks, finally an assessment is made of the financial regulatory and operational constraints to candidate countermeasures. Based on the results of the on-site requirements analysis, asset specific physical security countermeasures are applied to various points in and around the facility or asset to be protected. Selection of individual countermeasures is made based on an initial statement of system objectives and functional requirements such as detecting unauthorized entry and controlling access.

Finally individual countermeasures are selected by the designer and integrated into a cohesive protection solution. Preliminary cost estimates for the initial and expected total life cycle of the complete system are also established. Costs for those physical security countermeasures necessary to meet operational and vulnerability reduction objective are always a prime consideration for the designer.

Determining required protective measure: once the appropriate design basis threat parameters are selected for each asset, the designer is ready to determine required protective measures. The structured approach allows the designer to consider appropriate protective measures for each mode of attack, severity level and then consolidate them for each asset. Protective measures are normally divided by the designer into mutually supportive subsystem such as:

- Access entry control measures
- Detection measures
- Structural architectural measures
- Assessment surveillance measures
- Command, control and display requirements
- Operations and manpower considerations.

These mutually supportive subsystems are further defined by the designer teams of countermeasure application at the asset facility or site level. Asset specific measures are applied within the room housing the asset or within close proximity to an asset. Facility specific measures are those applied where assets are housed. Site specific measures are those applied between the facility and site perimeter.

Asset specific protective measures can include a wide range of countermeasure options architectural measures may include interior barriers combined with enhanced structural features that provide the desired level of protection. Detection and assessment measures may include a combination of point and area sensors along with duress alarms, CCTV surveillance assessment and area lighting. Interior control measures may include personnel access control within the facility and access restriction at or near the asset. Security personnel should be positioned to be available for response to intrusion attempts, while asset specific procedures may require the periodic check of asset locations by security patrols.

Multiple assets are usually housed in various locations within a facility. Common requirements among groups of assets make the designers job of protective design development much easier. When considering countermeasures for a group of assets within a facility, the designer should also consider other selection variables before arriving at specific measures. These variables might include the possible movement of the asset, local mission constraints environmental design criteria for establishing defensible space and acceptability of physical security options within the organization.

The process of compartmentalization allows the designer to define inner perimeters of a larger controlled space and build security measures inward from the points of access egress unique to the protection requirements of the asset. The perimeter typically will be defined by physical barriers through which access is monitored electronically. Within the facility, several compartment may be established within the common space to limit costly manpower allocation or to maximize electronic access control and detection through the creation of a single zone.

Groups of facilities that share a common boundary or perimeter require that the designer focus not only on the asset an individual facility, but also on the site. Generally sites with multiple facilities will have common or shared security requirements and some sites will even have a perimeter fence line and manned guard booth at an entry point to separate the area from the general public.

Countermeasures Cost Effectiveness

The designers consideration of countermeasures options will depend to a large extent on the cost effectiveness of individual countermeasures. Cost effectiveness criteria that might be used by the designer include operational restrictions nuisance alarm susceptibility, installation cost, maintenance cost, probability of detection, mean time between failure, contribution to manpower reduction, contribution to asset vulnerability and reduced risk, normally expressed in monetary consequence of loss or destruction.

While any one of these criteria may result in selection or rejection of countermeasures, alternative range of acceptable countermeasures must be linked together to form a system level impression of overall cost and effectiveness. Whether the designer considers either individual or collective countermeasures cost effectiveness, the following design issues must be analyzed.

Operational impact

- Lost through put time for identification alternatives (hrs/s)
- Estimated cost of physical reconfiguration
- Impact on safety and operational efficiency

Vulnerability reeducation potential

- Estimated saving due to reduction in known loss experience
- Increased reliability and coverage of physical security versus manpower
- Reduced risk of loss

Cost of operation

- Estimated installation and operations cost
- Estimated life cycle maintenance cost
- Contribution to overall organizational efficiency
- Savings in security manpower cost over life cycle of system.
- Ancillary advantages (eg use of fiber optic data link for voice data and other operational functions unrelated to security)

User confidence

- Nuisance alarm versus probability of detection
- Deterrence value versus perceived intrusiveness and inconvenience of countermeasures
- Acceptability of system approach for increased safety of users

Conclusion

The security designer must determine the appropriate protection to be afforded critical assets in the face of terrorist and other threats. Selection and ultimate integration of the various components subsystems in the design process is totally dependent upon a variety of resource and policy issues. Cost effective protective measures and their integration can only result from a structured decision process which considers the criticality of assets the capabilities of potential threats, the likely outcome of attack attempts, and the collective contribution of individual asset, facility and site protection strategies.

Designing Crime-free Environments

Reddy Atlas

Security is a topic on the minds and budgets of a growing number of clients, as is evidenced by the rapidly expanding supply of security technology products. The demand for more secure facilities, coupled with computerized technology is making access control and intrusion detection into a science of its own. Security needs for a building must be determined early, as part of the project programming and definition process. Burglary, industrial espionage, shoplifting, riots, vandalism, assault, rape, murder, and employee theft are crimes that endanger lives and drive up the cost of doing business. As crime increases, architects are being called upon to address security problems by incorporating security into the design and construction in all building types.

Designing without security in mind can lead to lawsuits, and expensive retrofitting with protection equipment, and the need for additional security personnel. If not properly planned for and installed, that equipment can distort important building design functions, add to security personnel costs, and result in exposed unsightly alarm system or blocked doors and windows.

It is primarily the client's responsibility to define the potential threats to people, property, information and to determine the level and cost of the protection that will be provided. The client may need a security specialist to clearly define the scope of security requirements in the programming phase.

Once the client and security professional identify the security concerns, the security system is designed to implement those objective. With the proliferation of security devices, along with rapid advances in system technology security planning requires specialists with a working knowledge of these technologies. Yet architects also must have a basic understanding of the principles of application and operation of security technology as well as an appreciation of the basic tenets of effective security programming. Any building must meet specific functional criteria, and from the function, the design evolves. A building must permit efficient job performance, meet the needs of the user, and protect the user from safety hazards and criminal acts that affect the production and service delivery of the building users.

Architects worry about the fortress mentality of security professionals while security professionals are concerned about the architect's failure to include security elements in the design of the building from the ground up. The conflict is not over whether to include security equipment in the building design. Rather, the conflict lies between a building's openness on one hand and control of access to it on the order hand.

Securing a building that was not originally planned to be secure is expensive. Architects have to sacrifice much more of a building's openness in retrofitting for security than they would if the facility had been designed for security from the outlet. Protection personnel and operating expenses are greater than they need to be because of a lack of forethought during the design of the facility. This condition is particularly evident in many of today's building, where modern design and materials have resulted in facilities that are especially vulnerable. Architects and designers can make the greatest contribution to meeting a projects security objective. Architects generally make the basic design decisions about circulation, access, building materials, fenestration, and many other features that can support or thwart overall security aims.

The environmental design approach to security recognizes the space's designated or redesignated use – which defines a solution compatible with that use. Good security design enhances the effective use of the space at the same time prevents crime. The emphasis in environmental security design falls on the design and use of space, a practice that deviates from the traditional predominantly on denying access to a crime target through physical or artificial barrier techniques such as locks, alarms fences, and gates. The traditional approach tends to overlook opportunities for natural access control and surveillance. Sometime the natural and normal user of the environment can accomplish the effects of mechanical hardening and surveillance.

Defining The Roles

Role of the client: is to define precisely the vulnerabilities and threats to people, information, and property (PIP); to assess the level and cost of protection and the coverage that will be provided; to develop the definition of security needs and provide the architect with a pragmatic description of protection requirements; to define who and what needs protection; to define the assists and the importance of each asset worth protecting.

Role of the security manger/consultant: is to help the client describe and elaborate the protection requirements and the level of protection required in each area; to help client assess the threats, security needs, and crime vulnerabilities; to help with the planning of access control, security zoning, target hardening, and surveillance systems. To define the basic security concepts with operational procedures and security manpower allocation, define the types location, and tasks of security personnel.

How does the security professional use the services of the

architects to the highest potential? The renovation, addition, or new construction of your place of business may require the security professional and owner to interface with the design professional in new and challenging ways. The security professional may be an employee of the business and responsible for many sectors of security and safety within that business. The architect or design professional will need many aspects of information from the owner client and security professional to develop the architectural program and design an efficient and secure building. The person that can provide critical information to the architect on security needs and procedures is typically the security director. If there exists no security director, then a trained security professional should be hired to provide that knowledge and assistance to the company and architect.

Role of the architect: It is to incorporate the security program information into effective space and circulation planning; to provide for clear sightlines for surveillance, and planned access controls at entrances and exits; to design for the appropriate location or sensitive or restricted areas; to design for the planned placement of security personnel; to provide architecture that uses design elements to closely coordinate security technology and personnel.

The architect can play a vital role in designing effective natural access control, surveillance, and territorial reinforcement strategies. Security design pose three challenges for architects:

- **Determining requirements:** Security needs must be determined early in the project's programming and problem definition stage. The design team should analyze the designated purpose of how the space or building will be used. The designated purpose will be clear when designers examine the cultural, legal, and physical definitions of what the prescribed, desired, and acceptable behaviors are in that space. The space can then be designed to support desired behaviors and the intended function of the space. The design team should inquire about existing policies and practices, so that this information will be integrated in programming process.

- **Knowing the technology:** Rapid substantial advances in the technology of security systems make keeping up – to – date a challenge. Many projects today, even routine ones, may involve security system specialists as parts of the team. As with other areas of specialization, architects must have a basic understanding of a security principle. Design professionals must be in a position to evaluate and implement technical security specialist and security equipment manufactures.
- **Understanding architectural implications:** Designs must integrate the complicated and sometimes conflicting goals of security and life-safe issues as well as other project variables and requirements. Space function must be planned to support the security objectives of detection, delay, and response to unwanted or criminal situations.

Designing for Security is a Process

To create a security master plan that can be incorporated into the architecture, a sequence of evaluations should be conducted before the security system design begins. These steps are outlined below.

Asset Definition

What are the vital assets-people information, property? What level of protection is needed for each area?

Threat Definition

What are the threats to each asset? Who are you protecting? Could threats be vandalism, espionage, burglary, theft assault, sabotage, robbery? How would threats be accomplished? When? Why? By whom? Where? What kind of attack or approach might be used to fit to the target? Are the threats highly probable, possible, or unlikely?

Vulnerability Analysis

Are the threats real or perceived? Compare the costs for the protection of each asset group with the cost of potential loss. Compare different kinds of security measures possible for protections of the assets.

Security Measures

There are three types of security measures available as a choice:

1. **Mechanical measures** —electronic security needs, access control, surveillance devices, technological solutions.
2. **Organizational features**—policies and procedures of staff, information flow and movement of people. The type, number and deployment of security personnel is the second choice.
3. **Natural features**—physical barriers, circulation patterns of people, information and products. Natural features include basic design decisions on circulation, access building materials, fenestration, and other design features to support the overall security goals.

What is Being Protected

One of the first steps in the threat and vulnerability analysis is to identify the assets to be protected. All assets can be sorted into the following categories. People, information and property.

People One asset for protection may be the human resources. The people needing protection may be employees, visitors, patrons, service providers, executive VIPs. The asset of humans is protection from assault, kidnapping, murder, robbery, terrorism. Failure to protect invited and uninvited guests on a property can be grounds for premises liability litigation.

Information The asset of information needs protection. Almost all businesses have vital information that could potentially cripple or destroy an operation. Computer records, blueprints. Financial information, proprietary secrets, personnel records, and accounting systems are the backbone of any business. Information protection is a critical element in a security plan. Knowing who has the information, where it is, when it is accessible, and how it could be compromised are critical issues to be designed for.

Property The asset of property needs protection. Property can refer to cars on a parking lot, airplane in a hanger, or office supplies in a closet. The threat analysis will help identify which property assets are to be protected. The architect can then use the security requirements identified into the design of the building, and incorporate into the whole building process.

In order to provide the information in a format that the architect can work effectively, the security professional should identify what are the corporate assets that are vital to protect. The three most common assets to businesses are 1. People 2. Information 3. Property. With any of three assets, the critical questions of a need assessment is:

Asking

Who are the users? (Visitors, staff, service crews, sales)
What can the users do in the building? (Tasks, work)
Why are the particular users there? (Official business, guests)
When do the users get there and leave? (Time, shift, patterns)
Where can users go to in the building? (Horizontal, vertical)
How can the users get there? (Access methods, circulation)

The security professional will need to be clear on the implications of each of the answers to these questions. It is recommended that a task summary can be prepared to give to the architect. The scenario development of asking the six key questions applies the same to a vice-president of a company or a janitorial cleaning service. The security professional will then determine the Security Implictions, and the Design Implications.

Taking the example of the janitor service, the Security Implications might be:

1. Control of after hour access.
2. Verification of cleaning employee status.
3. Security manpower to sign in and supervise entry and exit.
4. Key control.

These security concerns could then translate into Design Implications such as:

1. A sign-in desk for the service trades.

2. Design of access control system to allow staff to control entry log in movement.
3. Placement of garbage dumpsters.
4. Location of service elevator.
5. Location of service doors.
6. Alarm system for office and control room and deactivation.

These examples are just a small sample of the kinds of issues and concerns that need to be addressed by the architect based on information that the security professional has developed. The security professional must ask the right questions to develop security criteria. The architectural program or problem seeking stage should incorporate the information developed from answering the six questions. Later the information will be passed on to the problems solution stage of architecture. The schematic drawings, design development drawings, and construction documents.

Basis of Security Design-3D

The crime prevention through environmental design approach (CPT-ED) recognizes the building environments designated or redesignated use. The emphasis of security design falls on the design and use of space. This is a practice that is different from the traditional target hardening approach to crime prevention. Traditional target hardening, or fortressing, focuses predominately on denying access to crime target through physical or artificial barrier techniques such as locks, alarms, fences, and gates. The traditional approach tends to overlook opportunities for natural access control and surveillance. Sometimes the natural and normal uses of the environment can accomplish the same effects of mechanical hardening and surveillance.

Environment security design or CPTED is based on three function of human space;

Designation What is the purpose or intention that the space is used for?

Definition How is the space defined? What are the social, cultural, legal, psychological ways the space is defined?

Design Is the space defined to support prescribed or intended behaviors?

Crime Prevention through Environmental Design

Design professional can use three basic strategies for security design, also known as CPTED. They are natural access control, natural surveillance, and territorial reinforcement. Each of the strategies can be implemented through three methods: Mechanical, Natural, and Organized.

Natural access control strategies are indented to deny access to crime largest and to create a perception of risks to offenders. Access control is a design concept directed at reducing the opportunity and accessibility for crime. Organized methods of access control include security guards forces. Mechanical strategies include target hardening such as locks and card key systems. Windows may have protective glazing that withstands blows without breaking. Door and window hardware may have special material and mountings which make them hard to remove or temper with. Walls, floors, or doors may be specially reinforced in high security areas with materials that are difficult to penetrate. Neutral methods of access control make use of spatial definition and circulation patterns. An example of natural design is the use of security zoning. By dividing space into zones of differing security levels, such as unrestricted, controlled and restricted, sensitive areas can be more effectively protected. Effective access control is often the key to many security threats. Access control might be strongly considered in these areas:

- All entrances and exits to the site and building.
- Internal access points in restricted or controlled areas.
- Environmental and building features used to gain access (trees, ledges, skylights, balconies, window and tunnels).
- Security screening devices (guard stations, surveillance and identification equipment).

Surveillance strategies are design concepts directed at keeping intruders under observation. Organized surveillance strategies include police and guard patrols. Lighting and CCTV are mechanical strategies for surveillance, and natural strategies include windows, low landscaping, and raised entrances. Surveillance strategies are those directed at primarily keeping intruders under observation. Surveillance strategies include police and guard patrols. Lighting and CCTV are mechanical strategies for surveillance, and natural strategies include windows, low landscaping, and raised entrance.

Territorial reinforcement strategies involve creating or extending the sphere of influence. Territorial strategies suggest that physical design can create or extend the sphere of territorial influence so that users develop a sense of proprietorship. This sense of territorial influence can alert potential offenders that they don't belong there, that they are at risk of being seen and identified, and that their behavior will not be tolerated or go unreported. Natural access control and surveillance contribute to a sense of territorially, boosting security by encouraging users to protect their turf. Organized territorial strategies typically include neighborhood crime watches, receptionists, guard stations; mechanical strategies can be perimeter sensing systems;' natural territorial strategies include fences, walls, and landscaping.

CPTED security design process is applied on a macro to micro level. The three levels are site security design, building perimeter, and inner building space or point protection. Electronic intrusion detection, perimeter protection, and access control techniques must be elements in a total security system and design approach. Each technique has distinct technological and operational characteristics, and environmental reactions, along with differing requirements for installation and maintenance. In order to determine what security technology is the most cost effective and appropriate the following questions should be answered by the owner, architect, and competent security consultant:

1. **What is the system to be used for?** For example, is the system designed to prevent escape or intrusion; for high or low security profile security; provide for an interior or exterior system; what are the methods of responding to alarms? How long a delay from

criminal entry is desired? To justify the use of an electronic access control system, the client will need to know what areas and equipment are to be protected, and also what the potential loss or damages will cost. Each security situation is unique: there are no package solutions.

2. **What are the operational aspects of a security system that is required, and what is their priority?** The type of alarm system needs to be defined, as well as, the allowable false alarm rate tolerance. Inquiry is made on what is the proposed transmission system from sensors to alarms, for example radio waves, hard wired, dedicated circuits, multiplex system? What is the backup system in power and hardware? How are the alarms assessed for effectiveness, i.e. With CCTV, lights, horns, bells, or printed records? Does the system have tamper alarms, self tests or lightning protection? Each security system requires calls for careful forethought on the implementation and operation.
3. **What are the environmental impacts that effect the security system?** Examples of such conditions are weather, water surfaces, wildlife, vegetation and corrosive condition of acid rain or salt. Information is needed on topographic conditions of the site, are there any man –made impacts such as structure, traffic patterns, industry controls?

Site Security Design

Goal : What are you protecting? (PIP)

Threats: What are assets that warrant protection? How will attacks be initiated?

Strategies For Protection

1. **Access control solution: Control entry to site**

- Mechanical solution for detecting an intrusion i.e. electric sensors, microwave.
- Natural solutions designed to delay an intruder by creating barriers, i.e. walls fences, canals, thorn bushes.

- Organizational solutions allows patrol and ability to respond i.e. patrol roads, guard houses, watch towers.

2. Surveillance strategies: Watch for intruders unobstructed

- Mechanical solutions use technology to assist watching i.e. CCTV, exterior site lighting.
- Natural solution allows for the sitting of building to reduce blind spots and permit observation of movement by building users, i.e. window placement, location of entrances, walkways.
- Organizational solutions use assigned or remote observers to detect delay and respond to intruders. Observers can be police, security guards, or building users. The building design may have focus outward, for example to allow observation of parking lots or playgrounds.

3. Territorial Reinforcement Strategies: use the building design and ability of users to challenge who belongs on the property and if an intruder has a legitimate purpose.

- Mechanical solutions will define boundaries and territory with perimeter protection systems.
- Natural solutions will create boundaries with the building forms or landscaping to clearly delineate the public, semi-public, semi-private, and private spacers.
- Organized solutions will provide the staff and / or users of building to distinguish outsiders or violators from legitimate users of site. The site may have a vehicle control system that requires stickers, decals, ID cards, access control badges, or personnel verification.

Building Perimeter

Goal: To protect the building skin from violation of intruders.

Threat: What are threats? Is it criminals, explosions, terrorism, burglary?

Strategies For Protection:

1. **Access control strategies will control ingress and egress into the building.**

- Mechanical solutions will strengthen vulnerable points – doors, windows, utility openings, basements. i.e. locking system access control systems.
- Natural solutions will clearly define the entrance lobby, allow for careful placement of fire exits and design in control and surveillance of those doors. Material selections for glazing and wall construction will be consistent with threat level. Entrances may use sally ports or security vestibules for controlled entry.
- Organized solutions will design the coordinated placement of a receptionist, guard station, doorman, to permit screening.

2. **Surveillance strategies will allow building points to be observable by assigned and / or remote observers.**

- Mechanical solutions may use CCTV.
- Natural solutions will use design to avoid blind spots and avoiding circulation conflict.
- Organization solutions will allow security force and/or building users to watch unusual people movement.

Territorial reinforcement strategies will permit assigned security staff or building users to challenge intruders or users who are violating the building's definition or designations.

Volumetric Space Protection Or Point Protection

Goal: To protect a specific interior space, item, person, or object.
Threat: Threats could be from within, espionage; or from outside such as fire explosion, terrorism, or burglary.

Strategy For Protection Include

1. Access control for delaying entrance to areas that are defined as of limits. The use of security layering allows movement in facility

in an open, limited, or restricted basis. Access control will use mechanical, natural, and organization solutions.
2. Surveillance strategies.
3. Territorial strategies

Issues to Address with the Security Consultant

Site Planning

- Access
- Services delivery
- Circulation patterns
- Lighting quality and quantity
- Perimeter defense

Main Lobby

- Visitor control issues
- Building fire system location
- Reception guard kiosk design and equipment provisions
- Architectural security barrier design – turnstiles, glass enclosures, reception areas, etc.
- Retail tenant security adjacent to lobby areas
- Development of unobtrusive CCTV surveillance
- Controlling access into emergency stairwells adjacent to the main lobby
- After-hours access control into the main lobby
- Alarm monitoring of perimeter doors
- Main lobby lighting

Parking Garage

- Valet or self parking
- Public, private, or mixed use
- Segregated parking levels
- Executive parking security
- Need for and use of CCTV surveillance system, emergency signaling system, intercom system, and guard tour system

- Lighting issues, including type of lighting and number of foot candles to be provided

Loading Docks

- Amount of vehicular traffic flow expected
- Impact if any on street traffic or pedestrian walkways
- Storage of package and materials
- Distribution of deliverers throughout the building
- Development of necessary CCTV surveillance and intercom system
- Provision of remote door release controls

Emergency stairwells

- Restricting access or allowing use by the public for interfloor traffic
- Communication provisions in stairwells
- Emergency exit alarm devices on doors
- Alarm monitoring of the stairwells
- Access control into and out of the stairwells

Miscellaneous

- Elevator bank access control and architectural design
- Communication provisions in elevator vestibules on individual floors
- Public washrooms
- Mail services
- Deliveries
- Security in mechanical areas
- Door hardware for telephone, electrical, and storage closets
- Security for fuel and water storage areas
- Roof access
- Tunnel or skyway connections to other nearby buildings
- Plaza security—issues related to landscaping, lighting, and use unobtrusive surveillance systems

- Elevator cab communications devices

Building Tenant Security

- A comprehensive access control program to encompass elevator car access control requirements and individual floor access control measures
- Security measures for individual departments and operations that may have additional security requirements
- Executive floor security
- Receptionist workstations
- Boardroom or executive conference room access control issues
- Vestibule construction of freight elevator lobbies
- Console room design
- Secured storage areas, vaults, and safes within tenant space
- Closet space for security related equipment
- HAVC and power requirements for security operations

Major Systems

- Fire and life safety
- Public address
- CCTV surveillance
- Access control
- Alarm monitoring
- Radio -communication
- Emergency signaling
- Intercom
- Guard tour
- Door control
- Uninterrupted power supply

DESIGN GUIDELINES

- Place unsafe activities in safe areas
- Design the exterior of a structure so it is hard to climb
- Minimize the number of exterior openings at or below grade

- Protect all building openings against entry or attack
- Provide for extra conduit for growth and changes
- Design walls to resist penetration by intruders possibly using cars, hand tools, explosion, etc.
- Provide sufficient space in the lobby or entry areas for verification, identification and screening of users, i.e. sign-in desks, contraband detection equipment such as X-ray machines, and personal identification equipment.
- Provide adequate space for maintaining security equipment.
- Protect all utilities and control panels from disruption by unauthorized persons.
- Design elevators, stairways, and automated locking mechanisms not to compromise security during emergency evacuations.
- Design lighting for proper illumination in coordination with CCTV-reduce glare, increase view of field.
- Design perimeter to be well defined and supported by natural barriers such as landscaping, mechanical barriers such as walls, fences, buried sensors, motion sensors, proximity sensors, and by organizational methods such as guard patrol.

Summary

Keep records of the decision making process. The security design process is applicable to all buildings. Design in security with system expansion in mind. Always plan for an extra conduit. The architect should design for security now, or the owner will pay for it later at a much greater cost. The health safety and welfare of building users depends on good security planning and design.

As one can easily see, a lot of thought and money goes into making a building secure.

However, an architect cannot change human nature, and a lot of criminal acts will be perpetrated in spite of the best – laid plans.

Security systems come in many varieties, but crime is also not monolithic, Furthermore, it is ironic that the kind of crime that most people fear is not the kind which occurs most frequently. Stranger crimes-assault, murder, rape and robbery-are less common than white collar crime. Most criminals don't tote a gun. The terrorism of the 21st century will probably not be bombings, but industrial espionage, computer pilfering and destructing of records.

Can an architect play a part in preventing white – collar crime? Not in any concrete sense, but he or she can create an environment of safety, which fosters a sense of responsibility among employees and design limited and controlled access for easy accountability. In such an atmosphere, the employees will not accept behavior which is unethical and disruptive.

Finally, environmental design can never eliminate crime completely because it does not attack root causes. Architectural security design may only be responsible for shifting the pace where crime occurs, it remains easier to make a building secure than provide jobs for teenagers. Yet environmental control does go a long way toward making people feel better about their work environment, not to mention the cost effectiveness of building security.

The Security Survey

Richard H Poole

What is security survey?

A. Security survey is an assessment of the risk pertaining to a particular assignment. It highlights the particular physical security measures that are deemed necessary to lower or remove the risk factor on the assignment.

B. Physical security measures are by far the most important in any security plan. All other elements such as CCTV cameras, electronic alarm systems, intercom system or computers security are secondary and always reliant on a sound physical security plan. In other words no matter what equipment you decide to use, there are some more excellent equipment available in this age of technology so the physical security must be properly planned. No matter what the equipment, it must have a physical manpower support to monitor the equipment action in order to make it effective.

C. It is therefore an area that needs detailed planning and to do so users needs an experienced security professional to carry out an in-depth study of the threats and vulnerability of their business. This in depth study is often referred to as a risk assessment. The risk is a product of the threat and vulnerability and must be carefully analyzed and quantified before assessing the risk. Once the risk has been assessed it must be controlled. This is known as risk management. Obviously you cannot control all the identified risks. For example : An aircraft crashing on an office block or a petrol tanker crashing into a compound filled with the gas containers and exploding. These are acts of God and hopefully these risks the insurers will accept. It is this type of risk that helps justify the management of risk which further justifies the survey of the property of business.

D. Many companies including big blue chip multinationals all fall into the trap of leaving the risk assessment to the insurers. Naturally they will assess the risk without necessarily catering to the acts of God previously discussed or indeed the level of threat to the business. They will therefore cover the insurance, making sure that they do so with a profit. I would suggest therefore, that it may often be prudent after having risk assessment survey carried out that you persuade your board of directors to explore the possibility of a direct approach to the insurer at their level. For smaller companies on the other hand who are not quite ready to explore this avenue of approach, It may be worth to systematically attend to the risks that have been identified and by so doing reduce the risk and vulnerability which will reduce insurance premiums.

E. What is risk? In order to illustrate the point clearly a simple example is given. A company is storing gold coins in a fenced compounds in the countryside. What is the risk?

F. ?	= GOLD	*	FENCING
(RISK)	(THREAT)		(VULNERABILITY)

Therefore risk =100 *100= 10,000

But

If the gold coins are placed in Fort Knox the threat is minimal (0.1) and the vulnerability remains the same.

Therefore: Risk = 0.1*100=10

You can see from the illustration that a through security survey makes financial sense.

Security survey can be done for a number of reasons. Whatever the reasons may be the end product is to remove risk and RISK= THREAT *VULNERABILITY

It stands to reason therefore that threat factor within the risk is important. For example, if you were required to do a survey or risk assessment on a function to where a VIP was attending.

RISK = VIP * Place to be visited
(THREAT) (VULNERABILITY)

In this case if the VIP was required to move in a crowd which has not been searched or processed, the risk is greater than if the VIP was attending a function where all the attendees were by invitation only and where a facility existed to search the person and baggage of every guest.

The same simple formulae of assessing RISK from THREAT and VULNERABILITY applies to all areas of business.

In the world of modern technology, business are lending new avenues to explore the development of new products. The changing world of manufacturing techniques has a major impact on risk management. It is up to you the security manager, to keep abreast of what your company is doing and be prepared to carry put a security survey and make recommendations where necessary. To the outside world, the factory or business looks the same but the micro chip being manufactured for the latest computer or indeed the new computer that has been installed to safeguard the company secret effect risk. The micro chips can be stolen, copied and used elsewhere while company manufacturing secrets removed from a computers bank results in espionage. It is here that the security manager comes into his own and makes his position in the organization secure by recommending action to reduce the risk security measures which should meet and control the real risks of today, no more and no less.

How to Carry out a Security Survey

Let me start by stating the obvious- an in depth survey takes time and cannot be rushed. Areas cannot be overlooked because at face value they seem insignificant. You need a detailed and thorough knowledge of the potential threats. In order to obtain all the relevant information you need to ask certain questions. Examples of question you should ask are:

A. Who would be interested in what we manufacture and how we manufacture it?
B. Is there an alternative competitive product that can be manufactured?
C. Is there anybody who would want to stop us manufacturing the product by spoiling it?
D. Are we ourselves causing a threat to the environment pollution that would affect humans?

No single set of notes or question is going to make you into an expert overnight. Hopefully the guidelines I am putting across to you may help you to tackle your company security problems and even venture into areas where you have not ventured before and by so doing make a real financial contribution by saving your company money. By doing so you will not remain as an expensive overhead that certain quarters in your organization believe, is not contributing to total loss prevention or risk management. If left unattended, the problems will become bigger. Always be wary of the free risk assessments provided by insurers and brokers or even the local security equipment supplier. If you cannot do it yourself engage an unbiased professionals who will report the situation as it is and not as he feels you want to hear it. In UK we have RISK management companies who provide this type of service, who will give you the recommendations and leave you to advise your board of directors on the way ahead.

Industrial Espionage

I think it might be useful to explain to you in simple terms what industrial espionage is all about.

A. **The word Espionage** is derived from the French verb espier meaning to see something, intended to be created and the word espion, the spy. It has been a method to covertly gather information using the same basic principles for centuries with governments traditionally being the most active to defend their defence, economic and political infrastructure. The recent revolution in business, commerce and industry has meant that corporations frequently resort to espionage against competitors to enhance their corporate profit.

B. **Definition:** A good definition of industrial espionage is stealing, obtaining and transmitting through secret means of false pretences, information of industrial, commercial or political subversive purposes. In effect it is the obtaining of restricted company information from a company for gain.

C. **The Threat:** This espionage threat to business and industry is considerable and ranges from the hostile intelligence services, such as the Russian KGB to traditionally friendly countries making every effort to save money in a difficult economic situation and finally competitors. Its sometimes more cost effective to steal a product rather than buy or research, develop and produce. Companies also face an increasing threat from information brokerage, which is the selling of information.

D. **Industrial Espionage and The Law:** In UK several attempts have been made to introduce legislation protecting industrial information without success. Industrial espionage is not a crime because parliament regard the obtaining of information by a competitor as part of normal business practice. It may be that the actual act of acquiring commercial information may be illegal, for instance deception. Some laws affecting industrial espionage are:

   The European Communities Act 1972
   The Theft Act 1968
   The Official Secrets Act 1989
   The Copyrights and Corruption Act 1916
   The Wireless and Telegraphy act 1949

The Computer Misuse Act 1990

E. **Targets:** Most companies are in competition and most have information which is accessible through trade periodicals, papers and normal business contact. There is often information which is acquired in unauthorized manner. Examples are manufacturing progress marketing strategy, research and development.

F. **Methods:** The methods used by government intelligence agencies are frequently used by industrial spies. These include:
The employment of a trusted or subverted insider.
Interception of fixed and mobile telephone conversations.
Security were unaware of these losses for several months due to poor stock control, audit systems and these components were being sold under the counter. Engineers were programming the EPROMS with pirated commercial software in their laboratories and carrying out the chips in their pockets. The fiddle was only discovered when the Finance Directors son asked his father to get him some EPROMS from the company, that whole story unfolded. The estimated loss ran into tens of thousands of pounds. All because the security manager did not bother to get out and gather local intelligence.

G. Keeping alert with your eyes wide open can provide valuable information. Another useful tips is to watch the employee who is persistently late for work and is required to clock in. You will discover that when he is late he will take a route that is probably not known to you to get to his workplace.

Establishing Authority

A. One of the most difficult barriers to overcome when wanting to do a security survey is establishing you authority. Many departments will see you for the first time especially if you have not made it your business to get to know everybody on the site. Make an appointment with the manager concerned. Discuss with him you plans and tell him what you hope to achieve in improving the security in his area of responsibility within the business. With his cooperation, input and acceptance you are going to be able to achieve the information you require to carry out the survey.

B. When you are analyzing the data you have collected revisit the department, go through your assumption and recommendations with the manager and his key personal and seek their further advice and approval. You will find how helpful they will be and their local knowledge both on procedures and products will be invaluable.

To enter the premises and march around the corridors without leasing with the correct people will only frustrate and annoy the staff and build up resentment.

Finally, if you are aware that a particular area or department has had serious losses, your approach might need to be under cover. You must make every attempt to prevent a temporary cover up or cession of abnormal practices just because you are attempting to establish exactly what is going on.

Presentation of the Results of the Survey

A. Before you decide on how to present the results of your survey list out the areas of particular weakness in order of greatest risk or other priority.

B. The next step should be to look at the current system in place and by logical thought decide whether or not they are redundant, wholly or in part either because of new technology of because the threat has been removed.

C. Pay particular attention to the areas that you considered were low risk. Establish whether this is because the measures enforced are too sophisticated in relation to the threat or perhaps because other recommendations you intend to make, will remove the necessary for the current controls.

D. List the spare or redundant facilities and see if you can use them elsewhere. By doing so you can subtract from your list of additional and perhaps show a cost saving.

E. The next step is to map out the high and medium risk areas on a plan. Can any single or combined measure have the same effect in reducing risk. If this is the case then how do we get it done. Do we extend the perimeter fence or perhaps relocate a specific department?

F. A series of what it is will eventually enable a rationalism or the overall security plan. This time is well spent because when you enter the area of capital expenditure section, every group manager and financial advisor will be challenging your need by asking why and what we are doing this for.

   Spend time thinking through the problems and exploring every possible scenario. You will build your own confidence in the measures you intend to submit in your written report and eliminate the probing you will get from the overnight security experts you will encounter at the meeting.

G. The next conformation you can expect is with the insurers whether direct or via brokers, it is here that your report must be clear and balanced enough to demonstrate how the original risk and exposure has been considerably reduced with the implementations of your proposals. This reduction in risk should reduce the premiums. This will not be easy and you will have to fight hard with continuous reference to the competition. This positive approach by you will demonstrate that your company have tackled the problems of loss prevention control and have by so doing exercised a positive approach to risk management. This should generate a positive response from the insurers.

H. The insurers will want to review your security plan from time to time and may wish to have access to your regular surveys. I recommend that you go along with these proposals as it only adds strength to your position the time and effort put into your security survey will be both beneficial to security and cost effective to the company.

Protecting High Profile People

R K Sinha

The task of executive protection is becoming increasingly challenging and demanding day by day. The operatives make use of the latest technology and have developed worldwide ramifications through the nexus of terrorists, smugglers and gun runners. Their modus operandi is not sophisticated but has acquired deftness, dexterity and speed. Therefore, this challenge now calls for specialization with a high degree of professionalism.

Thousands of senior executives of the large number of corporations throughout the world, who are of any significance in the commercial world, have become vulnerable to the threat of executive protection. Similar is the plight of thousands of other high profile personalities, who have achieved excellence in their respective fields like arts and culture, music, sports, theatre, cinema, journalism or politics. Various terrorists and criminal groups know it very well that due to their significant position in the society, kidnapping of these executives and high profile personalities can fetch them handsome ransom money, wide media coverage and also might end up in jail. Terrorist indulge in these activities to create panic and to undermine the confidence of the people in the establishment.

The Threat

The threats which a normal high profile executives faces today are following:

1. Threat of physical assault or humiliation at work place by a violent mob of workers.
2. Threat of mental torture to self and family through anonymous calls and letters.
3. Threat of getting mugged while moving on the streets.
4. Threat of getting kidnapped and abducted for ransom or for black– mailing and
5. Threat of assassination.

An important point to note when we discuss about threat potential, the possibility of all the threats mentioned above also apply to the family members of the executive. Another interesting point to note is that as we raise the protection level of an executive, the probability of the family members becoming soft targets rises. The reason being that the moment a targeted executive becomes a difficult target due to increased level of protection; the attention is automatically shifted to the family members, who are likely to be less protected.

Reason for Increasing Threat

A number of reasons may be attributed to increased threat perception of the executives during the past few years. Some of the important reasons are as below:

1. Increasing Expectation.
2. Diminishing Loyalties.
3. General lawlessness.
4. Unemployment.
5. Terrorism.
6. Irresponsible trade unionism or political movements / disaffected employees.
7. Unethical competitors.
8. Disproportionate reasons and
9. Ineffective law enforcement.

Threatened Executive

People ask me how to identify a threatened executive. A threatened executive can be defined in the following words: "Any executive who is required to take such decisions on behalf of the country which may subsequently benefit or harm an individual or a group of people; whether workers or outsiders is a potentially threatened executive." However this is a general statement and this definition may vary according to situation. Therefore in executive protections, maximum weightage should be given by any protective agency to this identification of the threatened executive, the level of threat perception and the persons/ groups from whom the threat is anticipated.

Vulnerability

There are a number of vulnerable points in executive protection and a number of situations when even highly protected executives might become vulnerable or a soft target. The following few points are important to note:

1. Casualness at home and office.
2. Drive between home and office.
3. Check- points and bottlenecks.
4. Traveling executives.
5. School going children.
6. House wives when alone at home or while shopping and
7. Children in playground.

Case Studies: There are a number of interesting case studies from which we can draw lessons. However, I would like to discuss the following ten case studies involving five businessman, three political leaders and two diplomats:

1. Assassination of German businessman, Alfred Herrhausen on 30 November 1986.
2. Assassination of George Besse, president of Renault Car Company, on 17 November 1986.
3. Assassination of two former Prime Ministers, Indira Gandhi and Rajiv Gandhi and Lankan President Premadasa.

4. Assassination of Telco executives, Sahay and kidnapping of a TELCO executive, Pande.
5. Assassination of a tea garden owner, Surinder Paul.
6. Kidnapping and release of a Ranchi business executive, Harlalka.
7. Kidnapping and release of Mukesh Jain of Pasupati Acrylon, New Delhi.

Now let us discuss these case studies in brief with a view to draw some lessons:

Alfred Herrhausen

A renowned multi-billionaire German businessman. Alfred Herrhausen was killed while on way from his home to the office on 30th November, 1986.

It is important to note that Herrhausen was fully aware of the threat and had already taken possible precautions for his own protection and for the protection of his family. A custom built armored car was manufactured specially for the movement of Herrhausen. It cost a few million U. S. dollars. Best available commandos were deployed for the protection of Herrhausen and his family. When Herrhausen used to go out of his house, a pilot car moved ahead of his car and an escort car followed. In all the three vehicles, trained commandos with sophisticated arms were positioned.

In spite of the high level protection, Herrhausen was killed just 300 yards away from his home while he was driving to his office. Now, let us see how it happened.

Herrhausen lived in a very rich neighborhood and there was absolutely no scope of mounting any surveillance of his house or his movement. Therefore, the terrorist put one of its members under cover of a one man crew for road repairs six weeks in advance i.e. exactly on 18th October, 1986. This single member repair troop kept on repairing the road around the house of Herrhausen for almost six weeks till he was able to blow his car to pieces. The modus operandi of the entire operation was highly sophisticated and well planned.

There was a children's park about 300 yards away from Herrhausen's house which was a checkpoint. Herrhausen had to come to that point for taking the main road leading out of his residential colony. Now the same day when the single troop repair team arrived i.e. 18th October, 1986, a highly expensive children bicycle was thrown in the park almost on the flank of the road. Naturally, it attracted attention of the other children and even some passersby. They inspected the bicycle and found in its rack sack some video games, comics and toys, all crazy stuff which spoiled children of a rich parent would like to possess. Those who inspected the rack sack laughed and ignored treating it as an act of "crazy boys". The bicycle remained there for a few days and suddenly disappeared from the scene. Those who observed it again laughed. A couple of days later, the bicycle was again found thrown at the same place. This time people ignored it. Between 18th October, 1986 and 30th November, 1986, the bicycle was thrown and removed from that spot 8 to 10 times, till the people started completely ignoring it and the thrown bicycle had registered in everybody's mind as "a part of the environment of that spot".

On the morning of 30 November when Herrhausen took the turn at that point, his car was blown up by using a high powered explosive. The terrorist had connected it with the detonating device through the explosives in the rack sack and connected it with the detonating device through a photo electric beam switch which was operated through a remote control. As the pilot car of Herrhausen passed the spot and the car in which Herrhausen was sitting approached the spot, the single man crew operated the switch and established the contact between the remote and the photo electric cell placed in the rack sack. As the car of Herrhausen crossed the invisible beam the contact was broken and it detonated the explosive, blowing Herrhausen vehicle into pieces followed by a fire in the vehicle.

Lessons: An in-depth analysis of this case brings out the following lapses:

(a) Although Herrhausen level of protection was adequate, the intelligence feedback was non existent

(b) No one in the neighborhood including guards in the house of Herrhausen tried to check the bona fide of single man crew, especially when he was taking more time than required for the job and working long hours, even without visit of any supervisors for inspection during the six week period. No one even bothered to check with the city administration whether the repair was authorized by them.

(c) They all laughed on the abandoned bicycle. It did not arouse any body's suspicions especially when a rack sack of children's bicycle was only thrown and removed, a number of times only to make it acceptable as a part of the environment.

George Besse

The President of Renaults car company. George Besse was killed in his portico while he was about to get into the car in the morning of November 17, 1986. George Besse had a very routine life. After taking breakfast, he used to come out of the house and as a matter of habit, used to take a round of his beautiful garden before getting into the car. In the morning of November 17, 1986,when he was about to complete his round and turn toward his vehicle, a chauffeur already holding the gates open, a terrorist couple hiding in the bushes of Besse's garden shot him by a mini gun from a point blank range.

The terrorist group named "Action Direct" took responsibility for this killing. Almost five months later, during March 1987, a hide out of "Action Direct" was raided by the French police. As many as sixty well–edited video cassettes were recovered. One of them was on the life style and movement pattern of George Besse. Another cassette was related to a French General, who had also been killed by "Action Direct". However, 58 precious lives could be saved due to the recovery of these video cassettes.

Lessons: Lessons drawn from this assassination can be counted as under :

(a) Terrorist groups do make a very close observation of the lifestyle of the targeted executive. Therefore, if the intelligence network of the corporation is efficient, it can be detected and the surveillance mounted by the terrorist can be blown off.

(b) A threatened executive must not stick to his routine.

(c) Home, which a person considers as the safest place, is one of the most vulnerable places from the point of view of executive protection.

Assassination of Indira Gandhi, Prime Minister of India

It is a well known case and does not require any detailed description Gandhi was killed by her own guard with in her residence.

Lessons: I would only like to discuss the important lessons from this case:

(a) Gandhi was advised by the security agency not to keep the members of a certain religious community on her personal protection staff. Gandhi disregarded this advice as she felt that it would not be consistent with her ideal of secularism. The lesson drawn is that disregard of the advice of the security agency might lead to disaster.

(b) It has been established that there was distinct change in the life style of these guards for a couple of months before the assassination. For example, they used to move about in hired taxis and not use the transport provided by the government. They also started eating out more frequently; a few weeks before the assassination. The assassins and their collaborators were meeting regularly at secret hideouts and visiting places of their worships to renew their oath to kill Gandhi. The obvious lesson drawn is that there should be intensive surveillance on the personnel security staff and body guards of the executives and to be more specific; any change in their life style, spending pattern and associates must be taken notice of.

(c) On the morning of the attack the two bodyguards had managed to get the places of their assigned duty changed to vulnerable point on some special plea. As a result, both stationed themselves at the same place and supported each other in firings on Mrs. Gandhi. No security supervisor on duty had taken note of this change in their place of duty.

Assassination of Rajiv Gandhi

Former prime minister of India, Rajiv Gandhi was killed by a terrorist group, LTTE while going to address a public meeting on 21st May, 1991 at Sriperumbudur in Tamil Nadu. In this case a female member of a suicide squad of LTTE acted as a human bomb and while garlanding Gandhi, blew her and more than two dozen other people.

Lessons:

(a) Like in the case of George Besse, the terrorist group had minutely studied the movement pattern and public meetings of Gandhi, his politeness and warmth while accepting garlands and flowers, especially from women and children had been carefully observed and noted by the terrorist group and accordingly the assassination plot was planned.

(b) The natural weakness of political leader to mix with the crowd, disregarding the well established security restrictions was also exploited by the suicide squad.

(c) The organizers of the meeting are also to be blamed for not adhering to the prescribed security regulations for admitting party men into the inner cordon.

(d) The commission of enquiry had pinpointed the lapses and inadequacies in the security arrangements for the meetings. It has held that the threat perception of an individuals does not diminish after he demits his office. In this case, Gandhi was not covered by the special protection group when he ceased to be the Prime Minister. The SPG Act has since been amended to cover the former Prime Minister and their families for at least five years.

Assassination of Premadasa

President of Srilanka, J. Premadasa was killed while leading a rally in May of 1993. The case is still under investigation.

Lessons:

(a) It is reported that when Premdasa rally reached the crossing, there were other small rallies coming from different directions, wanting to merge into the main rally led by Premadasa. The security forces had stopped all other rallies and directed them to follow and merge with the rally of Premadasa to gain popularity and Premadasa did the same thing, ignoring advice of the security experts and in the process, Premdasa was killed by a member of the suicide squad of LTTE by a life human bomb.

(b) It has been learnt that a member of the suicide squad softened some member of the President's personnal staff through wine and women and it was he who was the human bomb.

Assasination of Sahay

Sahay, Dy. General Manager of Tata Engineering and locomotives Co.Limited was killed at his door step when he stopped his car at the gate of his bungalow and was about to get down to open the main gate.

Lessons: Places near the home are most vulnerable. The gate of entry should be kept open for the car to speed in without any hindrance. Also the gate must be closed as soon as the target car passes through it.

Kidnapping of Pande

Another Dy General Manager of Telco was kidnapped while he was attending a meeting in his office, however due to prompt action of Telco security personnel and the police, he was rescued within a few hours and his life could be saved.

Lesson: Bottleneck points are very vulnerable and it is advised that a pilot car should move ahead to clear bottleneck check points.

Kidnapping of Harlalaka

R S Harlalaka, a senior executive of USHA Industries Ltd. was kidnapped while traveling between his house and office. He was released after several days. It is understood that a handsome amount of ransom was paid for securing his release.

Lesson: Travelling between house and office is vulnerable patch and alertness and pre-cautions are needed as it is an easy task to find out routine movements like traveling between house and office. Routes and timings must also be changed periodically

Kidnapping of Mukesh Jain

Mukesh Jain, Managing Director Pashupati Acrylon LTD was kidnapped while he was getting out from his car in his own portico after returning from office to home. It is reported that he was kidnapped by some terrorist group of Punjab. It is also reported that the same terrorist followed his car as he went out of his office. After about 15kms drive between office and home, when the security guard opened the gate, the terrorist car also entered the house without any resistance. As Jain was getting out of the car he was abducted and whisked away. The security guard who tried to resist was killed on the spot. Jain was released after two weeks. He was held in forests and moved thousands of miles in truck and in captivity. It is reported that a huge ransom was paid to secure his release.

Lessons: Drivers must be trained to watch suspicious movement on the way and the car followers. Preferably, the threatened executive should himself drive so that he can see in the car rear view mirror, vehicles following or overtaking his vehicle.

Critical Areas

The critical threat areas are near home and office and while traveling between home and office. Some examples:

1. A German Businessman killed 300 yards from his home.
2. A French businessman assassinated at his door step.
3. A senior executive of TELCO at Jamshedpur killed in front of his house.
4. Another senior executive of TELCO kidnapped at his work place.
5. A US military officer killed 300 yards from his home.

6. A Colombian businessman was kidnapped 200 yards from his office.
7. A Romanian Diplomat kidnapped outside his residence.
8. An Indian businessman was abducted while getting down from his car in his own portico.
9. Gandhi was assassinated within her residence.

Precautions and Alertness

An executive cannot be protected by the security forces, if he himself is not aware of the threats and does not co-operate fully with the protective agencies.

Observations

Observations is an important aspect in executive protection. It is the responsibility of the security expert to ensure that the executives are trained to observe some of the following important areas:

1. Watch for disaffected employees.
2. Watch for abnormal movement near office / home.
3. Train family members to discuss abnormal incidents.
4. De-brief children periodically.
5. Establish identity of visitors and
6. Do not hesitate to take protective agencies into confidence.

Counter Measures

There are numerous counter measures in the area of executive protection. However, some, of the points which every security officer must keep in mind are:-

1. Periodically review of threat perception.
2. Evaluation of threat level.
3. Notify concerned executives to observe.
4. Train executives to observe.
5. Train PSO's to protect and not to fight and
6. Discourage arming of PSO's.

Dos and Don'ts

No exercise of executive protection can be successful, if the executives themselves do not adhere to the norms. Therefore the executives must be trained and advised to follow the minimum norms. Some of the Do's And Don'ts are mentioned below:

Do's: Executives are advised to follow the instructions as far as possible:

1. Evaluate and recognize security threats to self and family periodically as a matter of routine.
2. Trust your security manager / consultant and follow his advice religiously.
3. Take your family and children into confidence about the possibility of security threats.
4. Train children to observe the surroundings and debrief them regularly, discuss a few recent case studies with them in a manner that they become more cautious and better educated and not scared.
5. Brief children, female members to be alert while playing or shopping.
6. Maintain records of visitors and telephone calls received at your home and office. This record will be vital document for the investigators in case of any happening.
7. Train personnel staff, family members and servants to converse briefly on telephone and divulge no specific information about your travel plans or movements.
8. Train your driver to identify change in environment and to react quickly. Tell him what to look for.
9. Keep the doors locked while driving. Never give any lift on the way. Do not stop to help victims of an accident as it might be an ambush. Instead, inform the nearest police station.
10. Train driver and self in routine vehicle inspection before starting the vehicle. Check break pipes, tie rod ends, oil, water, tyres, locks, undercarriage, luggage boot, battery etc.
11. Keep on changing route and timing of driving to the work place.

Watch for any vehicle following, possible ambushes on the way, usual signs like traffic-jams on highways, deserted roads etc. Be careful at bottle necks and check points.

12. Maintain a low profile while traveling.
13. Search thoroughly and look for suspicious objects while checking into hotel room; ensure that the lock and key are working properly.
14. Keep in touch with family and office on daily basis while on tour. Remain calm and cool in case of emergency.

Don'ts: Executives are advised to avoid the following:

1. Never take security casually. Maximum lives have been lost due to this kind of approach only.
2. Don't hesitate in taking your security expert into confidence. Never ignore advice of your security expert.
3. Don't ignore an anonymous letter or call or caution signals given by family members and friends. Every feeder is important for executive protection.
4. Don't meet any unknown visitor at office or entertain any stranger at home, directly and without screening the stranger guests.
5. Do not encourage casual and informal talks on servants or family members unless the caller is very well known.
6. Avoid divulging information about travel plans, movements etc. on telephone.
7. Do not take into confidence even your driver or personal staff about timings and routes in advance.
8. Never be ignorant of the surroundings whether driving self or riding a chauffeur driven car.
9. Avoid things which might fully involve you while driving like listening to favorite music on high volume, reading newspaper, magazine or serious discussions with co- travelers.
10. Avoid publizing the programme of travel. You should only be known to the people who need to know it.
11. Do not pick up friendship with strangers while driving / traveling/ flying or in a new city.

12. Never visit localities which are not very well known while on tour. Avoid sidewalks and dark lanes.
13. Do not carry heavy cash while traveling.
14. Avoid keeping valuables in hotel room.
15. Do not panic in case of any emergency.
16. Do not try to resist or react violently while in hostage situation.

How To Learn Management From Your Wife

Sharu S Rangnekar

Like everybody else, I used to believe that management is something you learn in management institutions or Universities in 2 years full time or 3 years part time courses, leading to a degree or diploma and even after learning this, you have to get booster doses of management training to practice Management.

The idea that you can learn management from your wife came to me as a surprise. There was a foreign consultant visiting India when I was in ICI. He was installing new system of inventory control in various factories of ICI. I was made coordinator and I went with him to various factories. One of the factories was Indian Explosives at Gomia, which being an explosives factory was in the middle of a jungle. In the evening, we were sitting on the lawn of the guest house with nothing much to do. This gentleman opened a bottle of Scotch Whisky, which has a strange property of making friends from casual acquaintances by the time the level becomes half. We started exchanging confidences. Taking advantage of this I asked him, "How did you get this new idea of inventory control?" He said "Don't tell anybody, I got it from my wife." I was greatly surprised. I asked, "How did you get it from your wife"? He said, In every factory I went, there was a problem of inventory records. They had the bin cards, the stock record cards, account cards and even computers records, but nothing ever tallied with each other and nothing tallied with the actual stock.

So while people were thinking they had plenty of stock, they would have run-outs and while they were thinking they would have run outs, they had plenty of stocks. So people asked me why you don't make a fool–proof system. I was wondering what kind of system I can have, when I saw on my bed-side table in my bed room, a list of various items my wife keeps in the house for the kitchen, house cleaning etc. I thought I have been married for several years and there has never been a run–out in the house. So I asked my wife, "How do you do inventory control"? She said What do you mean? I said, "How do you ensure that so many items we have in the house do not run out of stock"? She said, very simple! See this bottle of cooking oil. When the level goes below this I replenish it, that's all! It struck me that most of the store keepers are men and that they won't understand this level. So I said, put a tape and when the level reaches the top of the tape, replenish. Secondly, I gave it a long name VISUAL CONTROL SYSTEM OF INVENTORY CONTROL, so that I can charge a reasonable fee. But frankly, the system is the same that my wife practices.

And I realized that the idea was right there, but instead of learning from my wife I was going to various institutes and universities! Since then, I have been looking at my wife – and as many wives as I can look at (at considerable personal risk, because my wife still does not believe that my interest is essentially a research interest!). And I found that several problems managers face at offices and factories are faced at home also and handled in much better way.

I shall be describing a few such incidents by which you can see how you can learn management from your wife. Frankly, these are not incidents: I am sure you have seen them, but you may not have noticed. It is like somebody seeing a fruit falling from a tree. What idea comes to his head? Is the fruit edible or not edible! Newton saw a fruit falling from a tree and asked himself two questions – very silly questions, we never ask such questions. First question: Why is the fruit moving? Why isn't it stationary? Second question: Why is it moving down and not up? Why did he ask such questions? Because he had the framework of Newton's First law of motion which states, "A body stays at rest or moves with uniform velocity – unless an external force is applied". He said here is the fruit with force applied! Why is it moving down and not up? Because the force is applied from below. Since everything falls on this earth, he said earth must be applying the force. So he discovered gravitation. He did not invent it, Gravitation was always there – but thousands of people, before and after Newton, when they saw a fruit falling from a tree they did not think of gravitation, they thought of the edibility of the fruit ! I am sure this is what happens to most of us when we see the housewife operating. We don't see the management behind it.

Basics of Management

First, let us look at the Basics of management. Management can be defined in many complex ways – but to me Management is very simple, It comprises of three basic tasks:

First: To identify your responsibility and get committed to them.

Second: To identify your resources and ultimately realize most important resource is yourself.

Third: To experiment with the resources.

The best example for this is: THE HOUSEWIFE.

Every girl as soon as she gets married, identifies her responsibilities and gets committed to it. Her responsibility is to convert a house into a home. A house is a piece of architecture. A home is a place where you get a psychological support, feeling of warmth and welcome. Who gives this? The house wife. That's why they say in Sanskrit: "*Gruham Gruhini – hinam Kantarat atirichyate*". (A house without a house wife is worse than a jungle). When a housewife is away from home for a few days, you immediately see the difference that takes place in the house. A housewife identifies this responsibility, gets committed to it and looks at her resources. In most cases, the main resource is the husband's income. I am sure all husbands have heard how inadequate that is! But don't worry, she has another resource: which is herself. See how she uses it. I am sure you have gone to many houses, somewhere the monthly income below a thousand rupees - - somewhere over 1 lakh. Have you ever seen the homeliness of the house depending on the income of the house – or As soon as you take a sip, from behind the door somebody asks you, do you care for a little more sugar? And you feel sweet without the sugar. In the high- income house the tea comes invariably in a tray with bone china crockery, silver cutlery, tea in a kettle, the milk in a jug, the sugar in a sugar pot,- it all comes as a five star service! But the whole thing comes so coldly that you almost expect a bill to follow!! The real warmth depends on the housewife and not on the quality of the tea.

How to Manage the Boss

Whenever I give my training program of time management, stress management, decision making; someone or the other comes to me during lunch time and asks me that you are talking about time management, stress management, decision making but these are not our problems. So I ask them "What is your problem?" He tells our problem is "How to manage the boss? I have very difficult boss." I tell them if you want to learn how to manage the boss – look at your wife. As you know that every man is the boss – traditionally, socially, statutorily on the day he gets married. But for how long? A friend of mine says he was the boss for three months. Nobody believes it. Whenever I meet married people, I ask the husbands "After marriage, how many of you have spent thousand rupees without checking with your wife? "Not one hand goes up. I ask the wives: "After marriage, how many times have you spent thousand rupees without checking with your husband?" They say" Always! Do you think these ornaments; silver utensils come in hundred rupees? But I don't tell him. If I tell him, he worries." In most cases, the money is earned by the husband – but he doesn't feel free to spend it. The wife can spend it for the simple reason – she has managed the boss!

How does she manages the boss? You can see the basic three point plan:

The first point is to manage his insecurity. What is insecurity? You look at a two year old child. He plays for five minutes and then checks if his mother is there or not. Again he plays for five minutes and again checks whether his mother is there or not. While he is playing, if you tell him that your mother has gone, he always gets panicky! Why? He feels insecure. The mother is the security point. Oh, you will say, what are you talking about? My boss is not two year old; he is a 42 year old, 52 year old or whatever may be his age, that two year old child is still there. Every human being is insecure and requires a security point and the wife provides the security point.

I had some education in America. Whenever I used to go there, I used to meet some class mates. The first question I always asked them was "How are you doing?" He used to say, " I am doing fairly well but I have a tough assignment. I hope I do it well otherwise I may lose my job and my wife may leave me." I asked again "What did you say"? He said, "Yes if I lose my job my wife may leave me." I told him that in India we never think that way. My wife will never leave me even if I want. He asked "How do you know." I told that I don't know how do I know but every Indian husband is sure the wife is not going to leave. When I came back I checked and I found that particularly the Hindu wives have a very good trick up their sleeve. One day of every year they observe a fast to get the same husband for seven more births. Whether they really get for seven more births or not God alone knows but can you see what this gives is security to the husband. He thinks that when this girl wants me for seven more births, at least in this birth she is not looking for an alternative. And this is how the insecurity of the husband is managed.

The second point is to manage his ego. Again you look at the housewife. When the children are making some trouble, she will suddenly shout; "If you make any more trouble, I will tell daddy". Daddy feels very good. Some women are even cleverer. My next door neighbor is a south Indian. Whenever I am in Bombay on a Sunday, I go to him and have cup of nice south Indian coffee. Whenever I am having coffee, the wife comes with a pilfer proof cap bottle and says, "Will you please open it"? The husband flexes his muscles and opens it. Last time I was in Singapore. I saw a contraption to open pilfer proof cap bottles. I got two of them and gave one to my wife and the other to my neighbor's wife. Next Sunday when I went there; I again saw neighbor wife's husband flexing his muscles. I asked her "What happened to the contraption"? She whispers "Keep quiet, you know, it is good to make him feel storming at least once a week. After fifty, it is essential. I am sure all of you have opened pilfer proof cap bottles. You think the wife cannot open. I also have a bottle opener but he feels very good. Let him do that and this is how his ego is managed".

In organizations, people go out of the way to hurt the ego of the boss. The other day I was sitting with the chairman of a company. The computer manager came, and said, "Sir, will you please sign here? The chairman asked "What is this?" "You won't understand, its about computer, just sign here." Chairman asked him to leave the paper on the table and said " When I understand I shall sign." Hurting the boss's ego is one of the worst habits some of the most intelligent managers have. I know one friend who handles the ego of his boss very well. He does all the correspondence himself. But once in a month, he goes to the boss and says " Boss, this is a very important letter. It has to go to the ministry. Your drafting is much better. I would like you to improve my draft". The boss asks him to leave the letter. The next day, he gets it back with improvements. What were the improvements? Where he has written 'although', boss makes it 'though'; where it is written 'till' boss makes it 'until', but the boss is quite happy. His reputation has spread.

When my friend got a new boss, the boss said to my friend "Mr Deshmukh, as far as I am concerned, no flattery. Ok" "Boss, there is one thing I like about you is you do not want any flattery. As you can see in managing ego, a little bit of flattery can be quite useful. Unfortunately most of us learn in our childhood that flattery is bad. My contention is what is wrong with flattery? As long as it is not used to cheat somebody."

A friend's daughter brings you a glass of water, what do you say? Oh, what a clever girl, what a great help to mother! You flatter her, why? Is it good for her development? Or when your wife wears a new sari, and asks you how does it look? Have you ever told her the truth. Not worth it. Isn't it? So you can see the use of flattery to manage the ego is one of the very important principles in management. You can see the housewife practicing it very systematically not only with the husband but also with the in-laws and everybody around her.

The third technique the wife uses to mange her husband is what I call management by attrition. In normal parlance, we call it nagging. I'll just give an example when TV was available in Bombay, my wife asked what about us having a TV? I said, no TV for us for three reasons. Number one it is very costly. Number two the programs are bound to be stupid. Number three the programs will be at the wrong time when the children are supposed to study. After a month my wife said you know the children are going to next door neighbour to see TV. I said that its neighbour's problem. Why should we worry? After another one month she said "You got bonus, how about TV?" I said "No TV. In the next six months, seven times I said no TV. Eighth time, it was enough.

There is another technique to expedite this, which I call the hydraulic pressure. As soon as you say no suddenly a couple of tears come and then you say, who says no, yes, yes have what you want. This hydraulic pressure is used very effectively to manage the husband.

Managing A Difficult Subordinate

Some say, well, we have no great problem in managing the boss but what about a difficult subordinate. He is a very intelligent chap but always very difficult to manage, always negative, non co-operative.

I don't know how to manage him. I always say, you want to see how the most difficult person in the world is managed, look at your wife. The most difficult person in the world to manage is a three year old child feeling jealous. Think of your own house, suppose the first born is a girl. First child, monthly birthdays are observed; a lot of pampering. After three years, a boy is born. Overnight focus changes to the boy. What happens to the girl. She feels neglected, throws tantrums, breaks things, and pinches the boy. What does the mother do? Mother does not tell the husband " Transfer this girl, she is very difficult." She calls the girl and says, you are now the big sister. This is your small little brother. We are going to bring him up. When I give him bath, you come and wash him. When I dry him, you apply talcum powder. In fifteen days, this three year old girl becomes deputy mother; very protective, very responsible, very affectionate. The mother used a simple technique; delegation, it is most effective to manage a difficult subordinate.

Delegation

But very few managers use delegation. They say, look at my subordinates, all these jokers. How can I delegate anything to them. They will spoil everything and make a mess. If you fear the subordinate may not do the job well, how to delegate to them, look at you wife. Look at how a teenage girl learns cooking. She goes to the mother one day and says Mummy, I want to make *sambher* today. Mother says all right. Only your father is going to eat so you make *sambher* but plan and check with me how much dal, one cup, how much water; one and half cup and a little more, how much spice; chilli, salt. We don't have recipes by weight like 85 gm. 40 gm. 30 gm. The girl shows the mother and put it. When the *sambher* is ready mother tells you, you know our daughter she has cooked *sambher* today, you better appreciate if you are an honest chap. You appreciate before tasting. She makes *sambher* 2/3/4 times. Now the mother says, you know how to make it, go ahead and make it but check for trouble in step two. If the colour is looking funny or if the dal is not cooking come and tell me.

After some time, the girl doesn't come and tell anything. What does the mother do? Step three; feedback system she goes to the kitchen presumably to do something else, but looks over the shoulder.

How is the *sambher* going? When she is satisfied that the daughter can cook as well as she can, she goes to step four; abdication. She says, next Sunday we have a party; this time you cook *sambher*.

You can see the four step process of delegation -plan and check, check in trouble, feedback system abdication. Every housewife uses it and that's how every girl learns cooking. Indian cooking you can't learn by reading recipe books. As you can see every girls learns it. If she is intelligent, learns in six months. If she has father's brains, takes three years.

Professionalism

This shows delegation can work with almost everybody. But the main problem of delegation is not the fear that the subordinate may not do the job well but the fear that the subordinate may do the job well. This is where we have to look at what I call the basic concept of professionalism. Many managers want to see that his subordinate cannot do everything that he can do. I ask a manager retiring the next day, who is going to succeed you. He says, one of my subordinates, I ask, how well will he do your job. He replies; about 70% why the remaining 30% is protected from him?

Now you look at a wife. Suppose your daughter is married in some of her place. Your friend visits there come back and say, you know I had a meal with your daughter. She cooks even better than you, your wife is happy. Why? She is a professional. The motto of professionalism is "*Sishyat Ichchhet Parajayam*" (desire defeat from your disciple). That is exactly the spirit your wife has and consequently she is not afraid of delegation.

Development of Subordinates

Many managers complain that they have problems in developing their subordinates. They say that the chaps who are experienced have no qualifications and the chaps who have qualifications have no experience; the chaps who have both have no initiative; nobody is developing. Although they are working with me for five years, there is no development. I tell them if you want to see how to develop people, look at your wife. Look at an 11- month old child walking with his mother's sari in its hand. Mother says, look here, you are a big boy now. Leave the sari and walk on your own. The child does not agree as he is afraid to fall She says, no you won't fall down. The child leaves the sari very diffidently. Takes one step; applause; another step; another applause; third step, the child falls down. What does the mother do? She goes and kicks the floor. She says, the child was walking beautifully; the stupid floor came in the ways. Can you see the principles of management involved? Number one show of confidence; you are a big boy now you can walk on your own. Second appreciation of efforts; applause at each step. Third and the most important; support in case of failure.

Now let us see how the manager tries to develop his subordinates. He goes to the subordinate and says, you know, this is very important. I want to do it myself but I have no time, so I have to give it to you but please don't make a mess. When the subordinate is doing it, the boss looks over his shoulder and says, " Is this the way you are doing it? Ok, carry on, carry on." When the subordinate makes a mess, the boss calls him and says, sit down, you have made a mess. Isn't it? Not your fault. My fault. Knowing you I should have never given it to you. Can you see the three mis-management principles? Number one where the mother shows confidence, boss shows diffidence. Second where the mother appreciates efforts, boss criticizes. Third where the mother gives support in case of failure, the boss condemns. As you can see, every child develops. What he learns between age zero and three, it cannot double in the rest of his life. He learns a complete language. You know how difficult it is to learn another language. He learns etiquettes and manners; he learns ethics. This is the best example of what is now called HRD, Human Resource Development.

Motivation

Another important problem in management is motivation. The best example of motivation is again the housewife herself. We talk of bonded labour, has anybody seen labour more bonded than the housewife? First she has to get up in the morning to get milk and she will be the last to go to bed. Holidays, Sunday's, festival days mean extra work. Everybody says extra dish required, today is a holiday. And the girl who works like this is not even born in that family; she was born somewhere else, brought up for 20 years. One fine morning, afternoon or evening, you throw some rice at her, get her into a house. Tell her; this is your house. It is a silly trick but it works within 20 days, when she starts talking of my house. She doesn't mean the house she has been for 20 years, but the house she has been for 20 days. This is what we call the sense of identity and we use our language to support it. In Sanskrit a man is called *grushastha,* a chap who stays in the house. A woman is called *grushini*, one who possesses the house. This feeling of ownership is very strong. Whenever the husband is transferred or promoted, he moves and probably move to a bigger flat, bigger house. He is happy. But look at his wife. She has tears in her eyes. Why she is leaving her house? There is no point in talking about the legal ownership. Every housewife feels she owns the house. That's why in Hindi we call her *gharwali.* Somebody asked me, what is the difference between ownership and belonging? I said every housewife owns the house, the husband belongs to it. This sense of identity is extremely important to create motivation.

The second aspect of motivation is the sense of importance. Every housewife believes she is very important. Without her, the house is going to collapse. In the first year or two after marriage, she may occasionally go to the maternal place. Then she doesn't want to go there. I am invited at various places; sometimes they write; please bring Mrs. Rangnekar along. The first time I was invited at Khatmandu, they wrote please bring Mrs. Rangnekar along. I told my wife. Why don't you come along? You are invited, she said, how can I come? Who is going to get milk in the morning? Do you think the children will get up in the morning to take milk? In fact, do you think they will get up at all? They put their alarm on, I have to put it off and wake them up. They never wake up with even their own alarm. And the servants have to be told the same things every day, otherwise they don't do anything. The children won't do that; the house will be in a mess. Unfortunately for her, the children heard this. They said, nothing doing mummy. You have to go.

For four days we were in Khatmandu. Every morning she would get up and say, let us put a trunk call to Bombay see what's happening. But thanks to telecommunications department, not even one call got through. Fifth day we returned to Bombay, reached home opened the lock. She was expecting the whole house would be in a mess but nothing was in a mess. But being a management expert I said, "Good we came on the fifth day. Another two days and the house would have collapsed." She was very happy. Always remember when our wife goes away for a few days, comes back and asks you how are things, don't say we all enjoyed, pull a long face and say we somehow managed She'll be happy, why hurt her sentiments and ego?

Process Happiness

Many managers keep on saying, unless there is a promotion, there can be no motivation. They say, we are stagnating here, some use even stronger words. We are rotting here for seven years. I say if you are rotting so long, you must be stinking by now. But they insist that. without promotion there can be no motivation. My next question is when you last promoted your wife to senior wife, Chief wife, General wife. Any loss of motivation have you noticed? As you know, Wife to mother is not a promotion, it is additional responsibilities. Mother to mother in-law is a demotion but your wife is not worried about it for the simple reason that she is looking for what we call the destination happiness.

In everybody's life there are two kinds of happiness. Whenever you are promoted, you reach a particular destination and look for the next destination. That is your destination happiness. But how much can it be in your life? After all one can expect four to six promotions in his life. Every time he is promoted, he may have one month, two months, at the most three months happiness in his life; which means about a year's happiness in the total working life of 35 of 40 years. What about the rest of the life? Is life a big desert with four or six oasis? No. There is happiness in life which Edward Do Bono calls the process happiness-happiness of achieving something. This is exactly the happiness you find the housewife enjoys developing each child and getting it into shape. The wife is not looking for destination happiness – she is looking for process happiness. Every child when he is born is a selfish, uncivilized creature, by the time he is three years old and starts going to school. By the time he is 23, he starts running his own life. This development of the child is the process of happiness, the achievement that every mother enjoys and this is an important aspect of motivation.

Authority Through Concern

The next aspect of management that everybody talks about is authority. Everybody says, in this stupid organization, I get lots of responsibilities but have no authority. I ask. "Look at your wife what authority does she have and how does she get it."
There are three sources of authority:

One is the hierarchical authority. The organization says, you are in charge of this division or department. If anybody doesn't behave, you can take disciplinary action but only if the personnel man is present. He says, but please uses tact which means never do it. So this is authority of hierarchy. As soon as it comes, it goes.

The second authority is the authority of expertise. If you are an expert in something, you have the authority. But these days it is difficult to get that authority particularly as the technology is changing. When the same machine was working for 30-40 years, everybody who worked with the machine had authority. But now the technology changes every ten years or even five years and many times the subordinates know more than the boss. Just like in every house, who is the TV expert? The youngest or the oldest?

The other day, I was watching TV with a friend of mine. The picture started flickering. My friend's wife got up to do something. Eight year old grandson came and said Grandma, you better not touch the TV, you will screw it up, if you have any problems tell me. He did something. The TV was alright. I remember when I was eight years old, there was no TV. A radio was bought and it was kept at a very high level because in those days everybody believed that if a child touched something, it would get spoiled. In fact if anything in the house got spoiled, we used to get slapped. You must have touched it otherwise how did it get spoiled. Today, even three year old, four year old children are allowed to operate TV. The result, not only do they have confidence but they have over confidence. When I was small, I used to believe father knows everything. Anything father doesn't know is not worth knowing. Today at breakfast table, my children ask me question. If I answer them correctly, there is a big merriment. They say even daddy knows. As you can see, the same thing happens in the office. When I walked into my first job as a 23 year old engineer, there was a 55 year old department head sitting. I said that this chap must be knowing a lot; he has worked for over thirty years. One day I want to occupy that chair. I hope I know that much. Today a 23 year old engineer walks in, looks at a 55 year old department head and says, what is this oldie doing here? He is half way to grave. And I don't think he knows any engineering. The engineering he learnt 30 years ago is all obsolete and I don't think he has read anything except his morning news paper. So the authority of expertise has become very difficult.

But there is a third authority that every housewife enjoys which I call the authority of concern. Just the other day, I saw in Bombay a young chap with a muffler around his neck. I asked him what is wrong with you; muffler around your neck! He said I have a sore throat. I said may be, but muffler around your neck in Bombay. He said I know it looks silly but what to do, my mother said. That if you don't wear it, she will worry. Not that she will issue a charge sheet for not obeying lawfully given orders.'She will worry', very important words.

The other day I was having an ad hoc party started without planning. Suddenly a friend of mine got up and said I must go home. I asked why?. He said, it is eight o'clock. I said it is eight o'clock only this time every day; what is there to worry about? He said, my wife is alone. I said as long as she is alone, why worry? He said she won't take dinner till I go home. I said she has the kitchen with her, she will eat something. Then he said she will worry. I told him to go; because he is going to spoil this party worrying about her worrying. Can you see this authority which I call the authority of concern that every housewife uses to control her husband and her children.

I am sure if you keep on looking around you, you will find many other problems like conflict management, generation handled at home. As soon as you have two children, the conflict starts but the wife manages that well. She calls the elder one and says, you know, the other one is younger you must take care of him. Then she calls the younger one and says, you know, he is the elder one. You must give him respect. So in spite of the conflict the children grow up with affection to each other. This is conflict management.

Similarly there is not one generation gap; there are two generation gaps in a family. But they all get managed. You must check how it is done. I am sure there are many other aspects of management you can learn if you keep on looking at your wife. But I must warn you. However much you learn management from your wife, you cannot be as good a manager as your wife because there is a biological difference between the human male and the female. I am sure there are a lot of differences you have already noticed, but I don't know whether this difference you have noticed. Which came to my notice just the other day when I was having a touch of flu? I was resting. My wife was having her rummy party in the next room. In between she came with a tablet, so I asked her, are all the girls gathered? She said, yes. Then why don't you start playing rummy? She said, we are playing rummy. But I said, you are talking. She said, we don't play rummy with our mouths, we play with our hands.

Then I realized that we men as soon as we get 13 cards to play rummy, we stop talking because we are thinking where are the duplicates, where are trios, which are the sequences, chances etc and while we are thinking, we can't talk but the women can talk whether they are thinking or not. If there are six women, they can all talk together. We men have a problem. If I am talking, you have to stop, if you are talking I have to stop. The women have no such problem and I found out why because the man is like a simple small computer single channel input or output or processing. But the female is a super computer several inputs, several outputs, several processing simultaneously. Now this is a very big difference and consequently you cannot be as good a manager as your wife. But subject to this handicap I am sure, you can learn a lot from your wife and I hope you do.

Image and Security Personnel

Renu Mattoo

When we moved into the house in which we live today, the gate had the legendary sign "Be ware of Dogs". "I've known you for so many years," I told the erstwhile residents, "but I have never noticed that sign before, nor seen any dogs in the house or compound."

"That is just the print." the ex-occupiers said. "You don't need to notice it but those who it was intended for did. That sign has kept away more unwanted callers than real dogs would have done!"

Yes, image does speak and it sends important signals. In this age everything is instant, sometimes the very first message that the image give becomes last and lasting impression.

In the security function, not only is it important to ensure security but also let it be known and where possible, seen that security is being maintained.

Thus, while an elaborate and effective security system will successfully foil an attempt to breach a bank or an industrial unit, information that such a system exists, will deter attempts.

Naturally, it is understood that while system details cannot be made public, the fact that an effective security system exists, not only can be, but should be made publicly known. Again while it is true that those are determined to break into a house, industrial unit or information system, will work hard to do so, the casual "Let's give it a shot here" violator will be checked by the knowledge that the security system installed is strong and difficult to crack.

Having said that let us talk about the image that is created in the public eye and mind by the personnel who man the security systems. What they look like, sound like and behave like can significantly add to or detract from the overall effectiveness of the system they represent.

What do they look like? Outside many establishments, private or public industrial or residential, the security personnel give great indication on their character, their pride, their job and seriousness of purpose merely by the way they are dressed. A uniform always adds great mileage to ones overall look, but a uniform that looks like it has been worn before, is crumpled, stained with buttons open or missing, shoes scruffy, bras dull, takes away everything that it stands for – smartness, identity with profession and a purpose and in this particular case of security personnel; responsibility and alertness.

Next, the posture and stance maintained during duty are a big indicator of the job as viewed by the incumbent. I remember being very impressed by the stone – like images of the guards at the Vatican, at Buckingham palace, and at Arlington, little children would walk up to these sentinels peer at them, tentatively touch them, laugh and joke around them and yet not be able to disturb the at-attention posture. These very people however come alive at the changing of duty.

I was impressed because I realized that only when you are fully alert, you can remain at attention for as long as those gentlemen did. It is so easy to slip into a casual and careless stance, with the weight shifting from one leg to another, the back bent in laziness, the arms either black or folded or being used for purpose other than maintaining attention. The statue–like pose by virtue of its lack of movement, may seem at first glance to be just that, a statue, but this was a security man who's also on guard.

The above is not to suggest that in all cases, a full attention posture is necessary. What is being suggested, very strongly, is that if a particular posture, stance or movement detracts from the look of attention and alertness then it must be actively controlled.

I wonder if it would be carrying the issue too far if I said that a sense of responsibility to the self and to ones job is also reflected in the way grooming of the person is undertaken. An unshaved face, untrimmed beard or hair, unscrubbed ears, dirty neck, uncared for the hands and nails, not only are most unpleasing to the eye, but spell carelessness in the mind of the viewer, extends beyond the person to the job. It can be dangerous if the viewer happens to be a prospective trespasser.

The look, of course is one thing, the style and content of communication is another.

Recently, we were looking for the house of a managing director of a company. We saw a guard on duty outside a particular bungalow and asked if that was the house of Mr. Meyer.

"I don't know," the guard replied.

"You mean you do not know whose house you are guarding?"

"No."

"Is there a lady children etc. in the house?"

"I don't know."

"So what are you doing here?"

"Duty!"

This particular guard is not a rare variety, on an impulse, my husband and I spoke to four other guards on that particular road. We got similar replies.

On other occasions, we have encountered security guard outside a private home dealing with a hawker in a most remarkable manner. The guard kept his voice low, looked the hawker in the eye and said clearly, firmly but politely, "Bhaiya, hum aapke baat samajhtey hai lekin, permit key bina aap andar nahi ja sakte hain" (Brother, I understand your position but you cannot be allowed without the permit). The hawker first pleaded, then started getting angry but the guard kept his cool and ensured that the building rules were not broken.

Can we teach our security personnel how to communicate so that they come across as knowledgeable, firm, courteous and very much in control, without having to resort to belligerence?

I do believe that for a security position, while height, build, health and fitness and in specific cases the management of weapons are important, the image creating parameters are not less significant.

Perhaps equal attention needs to be given to what impression those in positions of security create through their dress, posture, habits and communication.

Developing a Proposal for Security Services

Lauri A Kingsbury

What information is necessary in order to provide a security plan for a client? Can your company provide a plan so that a client has a clear understanding of his security needs? Will your plan clearly describe the extent and limitations of the services your company provides? These questions are at the center of effective proposals for providing security to a client.

A comprehensive proposal for security services is built on the foundation of a physical security analysis. In order for any security systems to be effective, it must be closely matched to the site itself, the users of that site, and the capacity of the security company to provide the services needed. An effective proposal evaluates the existing conditions at a site; the needs of those persons who work and visit that site; and the projected future needs of those persons. It clearly states the tasks that will be performed by the security company and the associated costs. A clearly articulated plan is essential for the integration of security needs and services into the daily work habits of the site users and the security team which protects them and their property.

This topic is of interest to security professionals as well as those persons responsible for selecting security companies. Security companies will be better able to market their services to prospective clients when they use this tested format for describing what they do and how they accomplish it.

When a security company offers its services to a client, those services must be presented in such a way that describes the manner, method and reasoning behind the recommended security measures. Security companies can accomplish this by preparing a Security Proposal, which contains a Scope of Work to be performed. When an organization solicits bids, they generally solicit bids via a Request for Proposal (RFP). In the first instance, the security company solicits the business of a client. In the second, the client is soliciting the business of one or more security providers. Proposals and Requests for Proposal s are interrelated – it is the initiator who determines the difference in form, content and method of presentation.

The first method is used for seeking out new clients or opportunities from an organization which does not require the formality of an obligation to answer a Request for Proposal. The following security proposal format has been used with great success and is offered to the members of the IISSM in the hope that they will consider it to their own use. Companies which require the services of security organizations may also use these guidelines to judge the services offered to them.

An effective Security Proposal clearly states what services your company provides. It answers the client's query regarding:

- Whether or not your firm has contacts in related security fields (e.g., if our company provides manpower; if you have contacts for hardware suppliers; etc.)
- How you evaluate a client (particularly the site at which the services will be provided) in terms of the services you can provide to them.
- What the scope and limitations of your services are.
- In addition, it describes what information is necessary for your

security company to evaluate and prepare this security plan; and illustrates the necessity for a client to have a clear understanding of the security needs of his organization. In short, a security proposal describes and defines the Scope of Work to be performed on behalf of a client.

A comprehensive proposal describes the plans for, the methodology and expected outcomes of security services. This is generally divided into fourteen phases (or steps). Some of these steps can be performed concurrently; other is dependent on the findings of preceding steps. Each of the phases will involve one or more of the following; meetings and consultations; site visits and inspections; research; preparation of detailed plans for equipment and personnel use; written reports regarding the findings and recommendations of the security company.

Security consultants provide research; organizational plans; criteria for sub-contracting; and other tasks related to overseeing the planning and implementation of security for a client. Security companies which specialize in specific aspects of the profession can tailor this format to meet their specific needs. Full-service security companies can use it to market the entire spectrum of their services. (It is a little obvious to state that every member of the profession relies on contacts who have the detailed knowledge specific to more technical aspects of equipment and personnel. Arrangements can be entered into with other companies who specialize in fire suppression, life safety, surveillance equipment, document storage and destruction, and the like.)

What follows is a detailed description of the fourteen phases. Not all fourteen steps may be necessary in every given proposal. The following format was developed, from a consultive viewpoint, for clients requiring evaluation of and recommendations for security services at locations of new construction; additions to existing sites; or substantial 'overhauls' of existing security at a site. Security companies which specialize in specific areas of the security profession can easily delete those phases which do not apply to them. In projects of this scope and magnitude, it is beneficial to group the phases into three separate stages. The first phase is preliminary. Stage One is made up of Phases 2-7, which are those steps necessary to the construction planning stage; stage two, performed during construction, encompasses phases 8-12; stage three, steps 13 & 14, are performed after construction and during occupancy.

Large projects can benefit from the use of certain project management techniques. GANTT charts (Named after their originator Henry Gantt) are essentially bar graphs plotted on a time line. They indicate planned start and stop times, as well as actual time spent. Many activities can be shown simultaneously on these charts. A major drawback to GANTT charts is that they fail to show relationships between tasks. They are best used when the time required for completion requires days or weeks, not hours.

The limitations of GANTT charts can be solved by the use of the two other scheduling methods: Critical Path Method (CPM) and Program Evolution and Review Technique (PERT). (Both of these techniques were developed by the project managers at the jet Propulsion Laboratory and the National Air and Space Agency to plan and monitor the United States' space program in the 1950's. They have since been adopted by a wide variety of industries.) Both methods will monitor resources, costs, quality, budgets, and interrelationships between the many different tasks necessary to large projects. Properly used, CPM will show the links between various steps of a project and the required sequence of steps. Some steps can be performed simultaneously; other is dependent on the completion prior activities. CPM assumes that the amount of time required to finish a task is known with certainty. PERT, however, can indicate three different times-to-completion: an optimistic time, the probable time, and a pessimistic estimate. PERT charts are referred to in Phase VII of this proposal format.

Organizations soliciting bids from service suppliers often use a RFP. The RFP provides a framework (or template) to the bidder. (Bidders are sometimes called vendors.) It describes and delineates the information needed by an organization in order to evaluate and compare bids. An RFP may also define terms and limitations to be imposed on all bidders. These terms give notice to a prospective bidder regarding hose services must be performed in the event that the contract is awarded. An outline of commonly-encountered RFP's will be provided to those attending this lecture.

The text of this model proposal is interspersed with explanatory comments. These comments are identified with "N.B" (nota Bene). These comments are for the reader and need not be included in the written proposal for the client. Model Security Services Proposal Format (for use by security companies to solicit a contract for services from a client)

Scope of work Performed for Development of a Comprehensive Security Program at (CLIENT(S) NAMES(S))

Phase I: Receive & review information from client in order to aid (security company name) in determining if we can be service.

Phase II: Data Collection begins.

The (Company) requests and receives information from [client(s), the Security Review Team & the Executive Review sCommittee (please refer to phase IV): architectural drawings, floor plans, blueprints, specification sheets, and other diagrams of the site & any structures planned for the site & any structures planned for the site and its cartilage; general description of persons who will work on or visit the site; proposed policy and procedure statements and manuals; other information as requested by the consultant.

Information pertinent to the project – statistical information; demographic data; current & intended land use; and other germane documentation is provided to the consultants. Data will also be gathered by the consultants from direct observations of the site and any research done by the consultants. Data collection will continue throughout the project.

Phase III: The Foreseeability & Crime Impact study:

This will provide a written report to the [client] detailing an assessment of the liability weaknesses of the site. Information sources include, but are not limited to, crime statistics and demographic studies. It will be cross referenced to the Design Analysis in Phase V, and the Physical Security Analysis provided in Phase VI

(N.B. Crime and other risks factors are of concern to companies throughout the world. The analysis of past patterns of risk and predictions of future risk, based on what has gone before, is an essential element in any proposed security project. In the United States, negligence and the potential liability arising from this negligence can be a major concern to the possessors and occupiers of land and properties. It is for this reason that projects of this nature address this aspect of the work. Issues of this nature are highly country- and location-specific. Please obtain professional legal opinions, specific to your company's country of operation regarding this aspect of security work.)

Phase IV: Security Review Team A Security Review Team (S.R.T.) will be formed to ensure the success of a security project of this scope. This Security Review Team will work with the consultants to: ensure that the goals of the project are met; act as a resource for the consultants; communicate security needs and concerns of the site users to the consultants; serve as the coordinating body between involved parties and the security consultants.

Membership on the S.R.T. shall be limited to seven individuals. One committee member and an alternate shall be chosen by the [Client] from the these function areas of the site: administration; support staff; financial; legal; maintenance; on-site security (if applicable).

One security consultant will be the seventh member of this team and the chairperson at all meetings. Alternates shall be kept informed of the results of team discussions and attend meetings in the event that a member is absent. If the size or complexity of the client site warrants, an Executive Review Committee (E.R.C.) can be formed in addition to the SRT. The purpose of this committee is to provide policy overview to the Security Review Team which is concerned solely with operational matters. Members of this committee shall be chosen by [ranking senior executive of client] and restricted to one executive- level representative from each of the involved parties: lead architectural firm; client/building lessors; Project Managers (if applicable); Building Contractor (s) (if applicable); building/site owner(s) Or governmental agencies (if applicable).

One security consultant shall be the last member of this committee and shall chair the meetings. No alternates shall be chosen. Meetings will be held every four to six weeks for the duration of the project, but will not be held unless all committee members are able to attend.

Phase V: Design Analysis.

This phase examines the plans & drawings for the site to determine how the design may contribute to the overall security of the site. Analysis will focus on: fencing configurations & styles; placement of lighting equipment & landscape materials; proposed berm size, configuration and placement; configuration and placement; configuration of roadway & other access points; and other design features pertinent to physical security. These features will be evaluated in terms of: how the design may contribute to the enhancement of security at the site; how the design may impose limitations on security at the site; and possible liability issues which may be inherent in the site itself and its design. A written report will be provided to the client. The Design Analysis will be cross-referenced to both the Foreseeability & Crime Impact Study in Phase III, as well as the Physical Security Analysis Provided in Phase VI of this project.

The design analysis phase is appropriate only to those projects where construction will take place or where redesign and remodeled of a structure is planned. Analysis can be performed for a client in terms of the limitations of the existing structures, landscaping and general physical configuration of an existing site where no construction is to take....

Recommendations and dis-cussion of existing limitations are important both to the client and to the security service.

Phase VI: Physical Security Analysis.
A Physical Security Analysis is defined as: "An on-site analysis and documentation of a location to determine the foreseeability of crime and the adequacy of existing physical security in order to establish a factual basis from which to make recommendations to reduce or remove the tangible opportunity for crime."

The analysis for this project will be based on:a) the architectural drawings for the site prior to any construction; b) information received via S.R.T. & E.R.C. meetings; c) the findings revealed during on-site inspections as well as research done by [Security Company].

The physical security analysis will be a written report which provides the following:

- An assessment of the probable security status and projected future needs of the site
- Details regarding the discovery of specific deficiencies in (planned or existing) access points (e.g. windows, doors, vents); locking devices; lighting equipment; intrusion detection systems; surveillance and observation systems (closed circuit television CCTV); fire protection/suppression devices.
- Specific recommendations for the alleviation and/or modification of these, deficiencies. These recommendations will include the identification, where appropriate, of types, grades, models, and in some instances, brand names of equipment
- Cost estimates for implementation. These estimates will include materials and labor.
- Legal considerations (if included in the proposal – please see note for phase III) will be referenced to the Foreseeability and Crime Impact Study provided in Phase III of this project.

Phase VII: Development of a Program Evaluation and Review Technique (PERT) chart for the security project.

This chart will allow the management of information for planning, scheduling, and controlling time in this project. The PERT chart will display the sequence of occurrence, dependent relationships, and estimated time durations for implementation. The consultants will develop and provide to the S.R.T. & E.R.C. PERT/GANNT/CPM charts which establish milestones for this project.

Phase VIII: Policy Development.

This step entails identification, development & writing of model policies which will pertain to site security; identification of other policies which have impact on site security; identification of priorities of the site and the site users which pertain to proposed security operations as communicated to the consultants through the S.R.T. & E.R.C. Model policy statements will be provided to the client.

The security company is expert in policy and procedure matters affecting the protection of people and assets at a site. Security plans and operations which operate ignorant of (or worse still, at odds with) a client's in-house policy and procedures, will enjoy little, if any, long term success. It is important for the security company to take leadership and develop these policies and procedures in direct consultation with the client if they do not have any in place.

Phase IX: Request(s) for Proposal.

Written Requests for Proposal (RFP's) will be developed to aid and support the management of [Client(s)] for the slection of vendors, suppliers and installers of equipment, hardware, etc. These documents will be provided to the client.

A model RFT will be provided to choose attending the lecture.

Phase X: Security Manpower.

These are eleven categories which are generally designated as "roles" for an individual working in the security field. This part of the study evaluates the proposed tasks performed by personnel assigned to security work and establishes benchmarks for the tasks that security personnel will perform in the future. These categories are: prevention; emergency services; protections; report writing; enforcement of internal procedures (and local ordinances if appropriate); inspection of premises; miscellaneous services; investigative work; administrative; and supervisory duties.

Identification and categorization of security tasks will be based on the functions performed by security personnel. These functions will then be compared to the analyzed needs of the site and the site users. Each category of personnel assignments will be defined using skills necessary to perform the job and/or tasks and measurable levels of competency required for that security position. This will also include a statement of recommendations for job descriptions.

Protection of people and assets is accomplished via security personnel. Equipment, of what ever technological complexity, serves and assists personnel. It does not replace them.

If necessary, equipment that will facilitate an individual's duties will also be recommended. Security assignments will be suggested for both security and non-security staff. Types and levels of training will be listed for both site users and security staff. Data will be gathered from: the Foresee ability and crime Impact Study; the Design Analysis; and, the results of the Physical Security Analysis. In addition, the proposed needs & expectations as expressed in S.R.T. & E.R.C. meetings; identified personnel responsibilities; a review of current/ existing contracts; existing and / or proposed procedures; standing orders; policy and procedures manuals; and other pertinent references will also be used as data sources.

These data sources will provide the information necessary to formulate a plan that best fits into the site itself and the site user "culture" for seamless assimilation into daily operations.

Phase XI: Vendor Selection. Bids will be solicited using the R.F.P's developed in Phase IX. The S.R.T. & E.R.C. will be actively involved in the vendor selection process.

Phase XII: Procedure Manuals.

Types and levels of procedures & training models for implementation on this site and model uses of these procedures will be written for (or provided to) both site users and security staff.

Phase XIII: Security Program Assimilation

The human element is the most critical component in the design & implementation of the security plan. To be successful, the plan must meet the needs and concerns of the site users without creating an undue burden on that user. Acculturation can be achieved through the efforts of the members of the S.R.T. & E.R.C. who are committed to training site users & encouraging their participations in the practices of security.

Phase XIV: Implementation of the Security Program

A follow-up Physical Security Analysis, as defined in Phase VI, will be conducted after construction is completed.

The [Security Company] will be available for several months on an ad hoc basis to the members of the S.R.T., E.R.C., and site users. The [Company] will be happy to provide informal evaluations of program implementations, answer questions & concerns, and troubleshoot potential problems for the users of this site. (This ends the descriptions of the different phases of a proposal of this kind.)

Limitations

Following the detailed description of the scope of work to be performed is a brief section describing the project limitations. The limitations section clearly sets forth those services which your firm WILL NOT provide to the client; those services provided by your company but not included in the proposal, or the limitation of these services which are outlined in the scope of work. It is highly recommended that this portion of your proposal document be reviewed by legal counsel knowledgeable in contract and related areas of law specific to the country where the work is to be performed. Unfounded assumptions which are not discovered or discussed can be fatal to business relationships. This is particularly pertinent to the security industry. The term security includes an extraordinary range of services and equipment. Effective proposals make specific mention of what is, and more importantly, what is not included in a scope of work.

Finished Appearance

A written proposal represents your company. The easier it is for a prospective client to locate pertinent information in your proposal, the better your company will be viewed by him. With this is mind, proposals of this length require certain style to encourage the prospective client to evaluate your proposal. A table of Contents, with page numbers, makes finding pertinent sections faster. Sections of the proposal will include (at a minimum): an executive's summary; the scope of work performed (the detailed description of the phases of work); results and limitations; a payment schedule; and, a list of prior projects (which can be contacted by the prospective client for references, testimonials and the like).

Proposals of this length and complexity can benefit from the inclusion of an Executive Summary. This summary precedes the in-depth, detailed description of the proposal itself and is designed to excite interest and summarize the full extent of the work to be performed. It should take the client only a few minutes to read it and decide whether or not to pass the proposal along to a member of the client company to evaluate the detailed contents of your proposal.

Clients require information and guidance regarding security. The security professionals are in the best position to fulfill this need. Understanding is reached when both parties operate from a common factual basis. This builds sounds foundation for long term and profitable business relationships. Without this dedication to provide this type of educational service, in addition to perusal and equipment, is ethical business practice. A professional which seeks to protect lives and property can do no less.

Total Quality Management: A People Building Journey

U K Chaubey

In the stiff competition both global and domestic, Total Quality Management (TQM) has now become a buzz word in the industries world. Customers have been demanding goods and services of a high quality. The term Quality itself has not remained static in its sweep and meaning but has been behaving like a moving point. Therefore, organizations have been trying to understand the meaning of TQM and then applying it for better and better results. For quite some time Statistical Quality Control (SQC) was confined to the quality of finished goods. The result was that in some organizations while the finished product was expected to be of a high order, other services like the staff functions, the services and maintenance etc could have continued to be handled in a slovenly manner. In this kind of situation it is natural that the organizations were not able to produce goods and services of a high quality over a period of time. Particularly in the United States of America in the 50s this subject was being discussed and debated in an intense manner. Dr D W Edwards Deming the Father of Modern Quality Movement (TQM) in the world, after studying the phenomenon of bad quality and after deep and long observation advised the industries and managers to view the subject of Quality in totality covering under its scope all the aspects of the functioning of an organization. However, the leaders of American industry did not bother much about the precepts being propounded by Dr Deming. More or less at the same time the Japanese were very keen to restructure their industries after the devastation of the Second World War.

On the advice of American government Dr Deming went to Japan where he lectured to the leaders of the industries and said that Quality should be viewed as a holistic concept covering the totality of the organization functioning. He further said that quality assurance cannot be achieved merely through inspections at the end of product process, because this involves double work and wastage of resources. He advised that the concept of quality should be built in the system itself so that quality assurance becomes the second nature of Workers, Supervisors and Managers. His observation was that 80% of the problems are caused by 20% of the causes. The causes are generally rooted in the system of production and management. The Industrialists and Scientists in Japan were much impressed by the exhortations of Dr Deming and they started implementing his advice in totality. Dr Deming was of the view that quality must come from Top Down i.e. the commitment of Chief Executive and top management is necessary because people should be at the centre of the movement.

New Management Philosophy

Dr Deming said that in order that quality movement is embraced by the rank and file, it is necessary that the following fourteen points must be accepted and implemented in totality.

1. **Create constancy of purpose for improvement of product and service.** Not only does Deming stress the need for a continuing emphasis on quality improvement, he also, more subtly, points out that quality, not profit, should be the primary purpose. Profit, for Deming, is a consequence, a by-product, of a management approach centered on quality.

2. **Adopt the new philosophy.** Here Deming reiterates the need for constancy of purpose while emphasizing how important it is for this purpose to be shared by everyone in the organization and inculcated like a philosophy, which it really is.
3. **Cease dependence on mass inspection.** Quality cannot be added on; it must be built in from the start. Mass inspection is completely off the mark. It assumes that quality can be achieved by identifying and then correcting errors. This means that workers are paid to make errors and are then paid again to correct them. This is not to say that workers like this any more than do managers. Deming notes that almost all workers want to do work of a high quality, work in which they can feel pride and a sense of accomplishment.
4. **End the practice of awarding business on price tag alone.** Deming does not advocate ignoring price when looking for suppliers. He only insists that price is a relatively minor factor, especially compared with the supplier's interest in and willingness to meet the customer's needs–that is the needs of the organization that purchases the supplies. (Those needs, of course, are driven in turn by the needs of the organization's clients and customers). The choice among suppliers should be based mostly on the quality of the materials they supply and on their willingness to work to improve that quality in the context of a long-term relationship.
5. **Improve constantly and forever the system of production and service.** This point restates management's never ending obligation to seek out ways to improve quality.
6. **Institute training.** Deming does not limit training to the use of statistical quality control and other tools for improving quality. He also means training in how to do the job. Many workers never get adequate training in doing the jobs for which they are responsible. In American industry, about 70% of all training dollars go for management education and development. Only 30% is spent on training for lower-level line employees, those who actually make products or deliver services. This imbalance

can not only lead to errors, it makes it more difficult for workers to figure out what management expects of the them. In Japan, the proportions of funds spent on training for workers and training for managers are approximately the reverse. In India also, perhaps the situation may be similar. To make TQM work, frontline employees must receive ongoing training.

7. **Institute leadership.** Being a leader is different from being a supervisor. Supervisors tell workers what to do and then watch to make sure they do it. They administer rewards and disciple as needed to ensure that employees comply with orders. In contrast, leaders assume that workers want to do the best job they can. At lower organizational level, the job of a leader is to assist workers by coaching and by arranging for training when needed. For top management, leadership means designing the system on the basis of TQM, applying strategic vision to build a TQM culture, and constantly and consistently modeling behavior that exemplifies the values that support such a culture.
8. **Drive out fear.** This is without a doubt one of the most important of Deming's points. In many organizations, people are afraid to speak up, to point out problems, or just to ask questions. Managers rule by fear, using either special favors or, more often, various punishments to make sure that workers do as they are told. People are sometimes fired for bringing a problem to the attention of management. A concern for quality requires that employees feel secure. High quality cannot be attained unless managers operate in a culture of openers, in which no one is afraid telling the truth, pointing out a problem, or trying to learn to do the job better may lead to the adverse consequences.
9. **Break down barriers between staff areas.** Traditional organizational structures encourage competition among units, departments, departments, divisions, and so on. But this makes it difficult, if not impossible, to work together to achieve quality. People in different areas and departments must understand that they have the same overriding goals, that they are in competition with other

organizations, not with their colleagues and coworkers.

10. **Eliminate slogans, Exhortations, and targets for the work force.** In this point, Deming is criticizing those who think that quality can come from motivation, from getting people all worked up through motivational speakers and inspirational tracts. This approach actually makes things worse in the long run, because even if workers really want to do better they still don't know how, they don't have the tools they need to improve, and they are not supported by the organization's culture. Deming has said that slogans and targets put people in the position of having an idea of where they want to go but no map of how to get there.

These days some consultants give impassioned speeches and create a lot of histrionics. One examples of such a consultant has been mentioned in the book Adversity Ouotient, written by Dr Paul G. Stoltz and is mentioned below:

"Ultimate Power with Freddy Savage boasted the marquis in front of the Phoenix Convention Center. This was the big event. I was guided to my seat by a member of Freddy's perfectly groomed entourage. At that moment, the rock music pounding through a Superdomesized sound system softened noticeably. A Master of Ceremonies took over the microphone on stage.

As he went through his introduction, I scanned the room. I saw the full range–individuals who later introduced themselves as students, professionals, entrepreneurs, and the temporarily unemployed–good, earnest people–executives, salespeople, children, retirees, laborers, homemakers, investing their hard-earned money for one reason–to find something they had lost along the ways their motivation. They sought an escape from the pervasive sense of helplessness that surrounded them. They wanted to feel good again. They wanted to feel in control. "Finally it's here, "The big moment you've all been waiting for. The sultan of Success, The Professor of Personal Power, The Monster of Motivation.... Freddeeeeee Saaavage!" The Crowd roared.

There he was, larger than life. Freddy Savage. He bounded across the stage and grabbed the microphone. "Yes!" his voice boomed forth.

"Yes!" The crowd roared back.

"Everybody up!" he demanded. All 2,000 people jumped to their feet. "Form groups of their feet. "Form groups of three now!" We formed groups of three. "Put one person in the middle. Go!" One person jumped in the middle. "Give that person a full body massage. Go!"

I found myself and some guy in a suit rubbing from head to toe a community college secretary we'd never met. "Does it feel good?" Feddy asked. "It feels good," the three-hundred people responded.

"No, does it feeeeel gooooood?" Freddy challenged.

"Oooooh! It feeeeels gooood!" 666 people bellowed.

"Take a seat," Freddy directed. Everyone sat.

"You are in charge of your own destiny. You are in control. "He paused as he flashed his million-dollar smile at his adoring fans. "You can fly with the buffalo, you can swim with the eagles, you can roam with the sharks" (or something like that). And so it went for eleven hours straight. I watched as 2,000 people from all walks of life soaked up every word. The energy was palpable. I had never seen so many hard-working individuals so completely energized at the end of an eleven-hour day. They were pumped! But were they changed?"

11. **Eliminate numerical quotas.** Quotas encourage people to ignore quality. The goal is to meet or exceed the quota at any cost and regardless of quality. Even when quality meets specifications, quotas can have hidden costs. For example, one department may produce its quota, but the products, while technically meeting specifications, may not meet the needs of the uses the output of the first as one important part of a larger product. The result will be continuing conflicts as well as the added costs of rework so that the first department" output is fit for use by the second department, its internal customer. Goals must focus on quality issues, not merely on numbers produced.
12. **Remove barriers to pride of workmanship.** Eliminate the annual rating or merit systems. Deming assumes that people want to do a good job, not a poor one. They need help in overcoming

such barriers as the poor quality of the materials they receive to work with, the poor quality of their equipment, and inadequate job management designed and supported system of operation is needed that allows all employees to do their jobs well, not one that tries to coerce performance from them. In the Indian context both group assessment and individual assessment would have to be blended together.

13. **Institute a vigorous program of education and improvement.** Deming does not downplay the need for everyone to have a thorough grounding in the tools and techniques of quality control. These tools are the language of quality. But he also points out that people must learn new ways of working together as terms and new behaviors that support the new management philosophy–the TQM culture.
14. **Take action to accomplish the transformation.** Everyone in the organization must work together to implement a quality culture. Top management in particular must focus on a strategy and a plan and take actions to put the plan into effect. Workers cannot be expected to do it on their own irrespective of the training they receive in the use of quality control tools and techniques. Only management can begin the process of getting the entire organization–management as well as workers to take the actions that result in a TQM culture.

These fourteen points are the basic elements in the Deming's new philosophy of management and constitute an organic whole of a TQM culture. They have to be applied in totality and at the same time. Otherwise the result may be counterproductive.

Creating Quality Assurance Frame Work

Quality assurance involves the following three aspects.

(a) **Counting**–tools, techniques and training in their use for analyzing, understanding, and solving quality problems.

(b) **Customers**–quality for the customers as a driving force and central concern

(c) **Culture**–shared values and beliefs, expressed by leaders, that define and support quality.

In a few organizations TQM has been taken to merely an understanding and implementing the seven tools of TQM namely: (a) Control Charts (b) Pareto Charts (c) Fishbone Diagram (d) Run Chart (e) Histogram (f) Scatter Diagram and (g) Flow Chart. This is what generally leads to the failure of TQM movement because TQM si not at all confined to the tools. The tools are meant to help implementation of the concepts of TQM through involvement and commitment of people is not generated to its highest pitch, TQM cannot be brought in just by mechanical application of the tools.

Therefore it is necessary to understand what TQM really means. According to Japanese industrial standard 28101–1981 Quality control is a system of means to economically produce goods or services which satisfy customer requirements.

From customer angle quality is fitness for use.

Thus TQM can be defined as under:

TQM means that the organization's culture is defined by and supports the constant attainment of customer satisfaction through an integrated system of tools, techniques and training, This involves the continuous improvement of organizational processes resulting in high quality products and services.

The application of tools leads to a proper understanding and application of the Deming's process namely Plan, Do, Check and Analyze (PDCA) leading to further improvements. Continuous application of tools generates self-efficacy, and self-confidence, and self-esteem results from doing and succeeding by recognizing that success was due to one's own action and not due to fare or chance.

In order therefore that the quality is in-built in the organizational process it is necessary that the quality check points are embedded in the process of the working of the organization. These quality check points are:

QC-I at the customers end. In other words where the customers accept the goods or services provided by the organization with joy and confidence in a sustained manner it will be deemed that the organization has a TQM culture. Otherwise, whatever the organization may do, it cannot say that infact it has implemented TQM. At this point the quality check can be done through customer survey and through other, reponses from the customers which the organizations may be getting continuously.

QC-II at the finishing and dispatch line from where the goods and services are handed over to the customer. Generally the organizations have concentrated all their effort in quality improvement at this point. This leads to a lot of rejection and then extra effort is required to correct the imbalance. Therefore in addition to QC-II, QC-III is required.

QC-III is located at the site of product or in the totality of work activity. In some organizations this is termed as Process Control. This is assured through constant use of QC charts or through Statistical Process Control (SPC). This is also assured by putting concentrated effort on the 20% of causes which lead to 80% of the problems.

QC-IV In addition to the above point it is very necessary to check the quality of incoming materials from vendors and suppliers. Where the incoming material is not of a high order, high quality cannot be assured.

QC-V Good result at QC-IV can be assured only if the design for product of input material, i.e. raw-materials, spare parts etc is as per the specifications laid down by the organizations where these would be utilized. This is why in a large number of organizations there are specialists to handle the quality problems in the organizations of their vendors and suppliers. It would be seen from the above that while the work flows from suppliers to the customers clock-wise, flow of quality check points is anti-clock-wise starting from QC-I.

Quality can be assured if the model prepared by Dr Juran another American Quality expert is followed : Juran's road map to high quality involves :

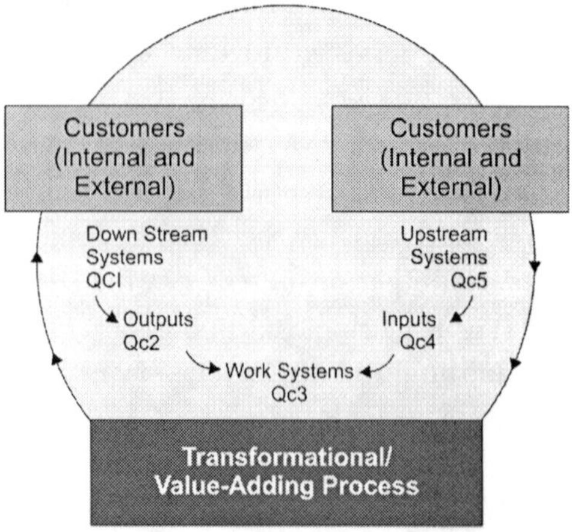

Step 1: Ask, "Who are our customers? Executives, Managers and Employees must first step back and ask who the customer is. They must make a list and then talk to people on the list to see whether they have identified the right people and to ask whether important customers have been left off. This will lead to the concept of both internal as well as external customer.

Step 2: Ask Customers, "What do you want and need?" Customers' needs and desires are listed and explored in detail. The list reviewed with other customers to see whether it is correct and complete.

Step 3: Ask, "What do these needs mean to us" The needs and desires that customers describe are translated into product and service terms that are meaningful to people within the organization. Again, a list is made. This list is reviewed with employees, modified as needed, translated, and checked for accuracy with customers.

Step 4: Ask, "What are the characteristics of a product/service that satisfies these needs?" Executives, managers, and employees throughout the organization must prepare the list of customer needs and identify the specific characteristics of products of services that meet them. Again, these product of service descriptions must be checked with customers.

Step 5: Ask, "How do we make this product?" Or ask, "How do we deliver this service?" Actual plans for making products or delivering services are developed in writing and in detail. Those who must carry out the plans are involved from the start. The who must carry out the plans are involved from the start. The plans are shared widely throughout the organization. The focus is always on the question, "How do we do it right the first time?"

Step 6: Put the plans into operation. After carrying out the plans, check back with customers to make sure that the products or services have actually satisfied customers' needs. An emphasis on measurement must be present throughout this sex-step process for building customers' needs into the system of organization functioning. What's more, the process is not a one-time-only event. It must be repeated again and again. These six steps can be applied in service organizations as well. In fact in service organizations, it may be relatively more convenient to do it, because in such organizations delighting the customers has to be done mainly through the application of knowledge, skills, attitude, innovation and disciplined behavior.

TQM Culture

In order that a TQM culture is embedded in the working of a orga-nization, the following eight crucial elements of TQM culture must be followed scrupulously in a holistic manner:

Culture Element 1 Quality information must be used for improvement, not to judge or control people.
Culture Element 2 Authority must be equal to responsibility.
Culture Element 3 There must be rewards for results.
Culture Element 4 Cooperation, not competition, must be the basis for working together.
Culture Element 5 Employees must have secure jobs.
Culture Element 6 There must be a climate of fairness.
Culture Element 7 Compensation should be equitable.
Culture Element 8 Employees should have an ownership stake.

The above elements of TQM culture mentioned above are self explanatory and can be easily understood by the people of almost all the organizations.

The eight crucial elements of TQM culture mentioned above are basically applicable more or less to all the organizations. However, infact there are very few organizations which have all the cultural elements mentioned above. These would have to be integrated with the basic management philosophy shown in the fourteen points of Deming mentioned earlier in this paper. This is why the cultural elements are so crucial because people in general would believe in a particular type of culture only if it is reflected through the activities of the top management. Where these cultural elements are propagated only through Lectures, Banners and others signs without being reflected in the activities of the management including supervisors etc., the employees in general respond by being indifferent or even alienated with the exhortations. This is so because culture is the cumulative perception of how the organization treats people and how people expect to treat one another. It is based on consistent and persistent management action as seen by employees, vendors and customers.

TQM culture can be created and sustained if the organizations have the following elements.

- Action that develop trust, such as sharing useful information and making good on commitments.
- Acting consistently, so that employees are not surprised or taken aback by unexpected management actions or decisions.
- Being scrupulously truthful and avoiding so called white lies and actions designed to manipulate others by giving a certain (false) impression.
- Demonstrating integrity by keeping confidences and observing basic ethical guidelines to show one's concern for others.
- Meeting with one's employees to discuss and define exactly what is expected of them.
- Making sure that people are treated equitably, that is, giving equivalent rewards for similar performance by different employees and avoiding actual or apparent special treatment for favorites.

- Giving employees meaningful influence over decisions about their own work, especially how to accomplish their work goals and what to do about work problems.
- Adhering to clear standards that are seen as just and reasonable, for example, not giving praise out of proportion to accomplishments or imposing penalties disproportionate to an offence.
- Demonstrating respect towards employees, showing by actions that one really cares about others and recognizes their strengths and contributions following due process, that is, procedures that are open to public scrutiny and that permit everyone to participate actively in their application

Leaders' Role

In this, the role of leader is really crucial, the leader has to be a designer, a steward and a teacher. He ahs to first design the system, process, and procedures which lead to a TQM culture. Then he has to lead various levels of employees into implementing this culture and then he has to be a teacher coaching the employees as to how do it progressively better. This is the kind of leadership which transforms organizations in which it is a joy to work transforms organizations in which it is a joy to work and where self fulfillment is generated through performance.

The Security Needs of Archaeological and Cultural Sites

A Kingsbury

The principles of physical security are the same no matter what the site or its location. The protection of historical, cultural and archaeological treasures is an area for the growth of security services. This growth area must be approached carefully and respectfully, ever mindful that historical, cultural and archaeological locations have importance beyond that of revenue and profit. The needs of these particular places impose a larger set of considerations for the security profession.

Categories of Sites

Sites can be classified into three general categories. A site may be of historical importance. These are locations where an event of importance or considerable influence occurred at some time in the past. Battlefields are the easiest example for locations of historical importance. Locations of significant [political] declarations or other events instrumental in the development of a cultural nation also have historical importance. Sites can have cultural importance. These locations embody a particular style of social and artistic expression that is unique to a particular society or class.

Culturally, important sites exhibit characteristics of a particular community or population. War memorials, monuments and other structures which celebrate events or commemorate a country's leaders may not be located on ground where a specific event took place, but nevertheless are a manifestation of that which a country holds important. These places reflect deeply held beliefs and show reverence for the heritage of a people. Museums protect artefacts (paintings, sculpture, other art works); libraries preserve documents. (Museum and library security are already recognized sub specialties within the security field.) The security for Cultural and historical sites must take into consideration the requirements of the users and visitors to that site as well as preserving the integrity of the site, its buildings and their contents for future visitors. Both historical and cultural sites are often actively in use. People work at or visit libraries and museums daily. Battle sites, Parliament buildings and other historically important locations can be places where people live and work amid the peope who may be tourists and curious visitors. Archaeological sites are different from the first two categories. They often are not occupied or used. Archaeology concerns itself with "The systematic recovery and study of material evidence, such as graves, buildings, tools, and pottery, remaining from past human life and culture."

Security at an archaeological site must protect this "material evidence" in order that study and recovery may continue. Archaeological sites pose certain problems for security solely because of their location. Excavations may be located in areas remote from power supplies or in the middle of a city with millions in population. The location of archaeological sites imposes particular restrictions on the selection and implementation of security measures. It can be difficult to place a location into just one category. A battlefield has historical importance–yet that battle and the events resulting from it have long-lasting cultural importance. Archaeological excavations may reveal hitherto unknown cities, thus altering and augmenting the historical record. A culturally important monument or building may be located at a site where historically significant events once took place. The boundaries of these three categories are neither clear nor definite. It is not the purpose of the security profession to provide a classification system for treasured sites. It is important for the security field to recognize that these three general categories exist; that sites will fall into one or more of these categories; and that each category determines, in part, the manner and method of the security measures chosen to protect and preserve that location. Considering the security needs of a site in terms of these three categories helps to reveal those features deemed most important to that site; those activities most likely to take place at that site; and the importance of the site to people holding it in high regard. The Need for Careful Evaluation Security services can be supplied to and implemented at a site at any time, with or without an evaluation. If implementation takes place prior to a formal evaluation, the security measures that are put into place may not be appropriate to that location.

The risk factors specific to the site are identified during the evaluation and analysis process. An in-depth evaluation prior to implementation is vital to both the initial and continued success of security at these sites. Evaluation will reveal both what has happened at a site in the immediate past and what is happening in the present. This knowledge is instrumental in making predictions on what security needs exists so that the proper measures can be put into place. The client almost always lacks the expertise in the ways and hows of security and, therefore, relies on security professionals to tell him what the needs are for a site.

Risk factors, particularly those risks internal to a site, will be revealed in the course of the evaluation so that sound decisions can be made for both the success of the security company and the continued protection and preservation of the treasured location. When a location has cultural, historical or archaeological value, the manner of assessing it in terms of physical security deepens. A manufacturing plant can be rebuilt. An office complex can be relocated. This is not true for sites deemed to have historical, cultural or archaeological value. A fundamental aspect of these sites is that they cannot be replaced or reproduced. Because of the profound connection between past events and present practices, there are inherent pressures at these sites which must be kept in mind at all times.

Religious sites attract many types of people. Most obviously, theses locations attract the adherents of the faith celebrated at and symbolized by the site. Seekers as well as the curious may be part of the throngs of people here. The great art and architecture created by the faithful and which symbolizes a religion, appeals to scholars and tourists alike. Crowds may attract the independent actions by a few people that are decidedly not sanctioned by and very often contrary to the beliefs symbolized at the site.

Action against large crowds of people draw public attention and widespread attention may be primary purpose of those engaging in these independent actions. The believers, the curious, scholars and tourists may unwittingly become bait for the disruptive or violent actions of those wishing to make an attention-grabbing statement that will receive wide media converge. Civil disobedience at religious sites has a long history. These actions may take either a non-violent or violent form. Protesters may be adherents of the faith or those in opposition. The problem posed to security be civil disobedience, whether peaceful or not, is two-fold.

The demonstrations themselves are a concern, but the fact that such behavior is often unpredictable, even within the context of past activity patterns, can be a constant source of worry to security personnel who must preserve and protect that place. As a side note of some interest, some archaeological sites may be the present location for worship by adherents of ancient faiths. This specific factor must be kept in mind when evaluating archaeological (and even some paleontological) sites. Security measures which limit access may suffer vandalism or outright destruction by worshipers who have celebrated their faith here for centuries and regard access may suffer vandalism or outright destruction by worshipers who have celebrated their faith here for centuries and regards access control measures as interference if not desecration. Politics is another inherent pressure, best distinguished by its fluidity and rapidity of change. At the simplest level, political entities may control ownership or regulate who is responsible for the operations at a site. Members of political bodies may initiate public discussion, using as a centerpiece a location with historical, archaeological or religious importance. Time and talk are devoted to the importance of a site, but there may be little that ensure. Debate can centre around the importance, the irreplaceability, the beauty of a site.

Political discussion can raise false expectations of funding; release hitherto concealed ill-feelings; increase (or decrease) popularity. Many sites are dependent on public funding for the for the costs of operation, but funding directly connected to current political opinion may not be the most stable source of monetary support. The last pressure inherent at these sites Is the mundane one of monetary considerations. Sites that are dependent on public funding may find themselves without a budget. The fluidity of politics, particularly when politics dictate funding allocations, creates monetary pressures. Initial capital may flow from political discussion, but continued support for long-term operations may not be certain. Even within the private sector, security it not considered a 'revenue-generating' area, even though its measures maintain and preserve the integrity of a site so business, worship, study and tourism can continue without interruption. Security budgets can be one of the first to be reduced or eliminated when funding grows short. Yet without security, daily operations may suffer, resulting in more lost revenue. No matter what the source is for funding at these sites, an important aspect of monetary pressure is that, whether public or private, the source will want "the most for the cheapest".

The desires underlying funding decisions may not necessarily be for the long-term good of the site, but only how much can be bought for as little a sum as possible. Background Influences Operating closer to the surface and thus more easily scrutinized are the various influences forming substructure on which security on which security can be built. These influences are part of the research conducted prior to a physical security analysis so that these findings can be placed in their proper context. At these sites, they may have more importance than at those places where security is traditionally implemented (industrial sites, offices, institutions, etc.). The presence of these influences and the manner in which they combine will determine which measures are selected; the extent to which security will be deemed 'successful'; and, the manner in which security personnel respond to events which occur at a site.

The question of jurisdiction is of paramount concern to security. Jurisdiction determines who is responsible for response to incidents, who is the primary protection agency at a site, who has authority over hours of operation and who may or may not grant permission to enter all relate to the question of jurisdiction. These sites have economic value to their region. Sites themselves generate revenue from admission fees. Businesses develop to cater to visitors restaurants, hotels and inns, craft shops and the like may become an attraction in and of themselves. Geography influences accessibility and traffic. Some historical, cultural and Archeological sites are located in areas that are either remote or difficult of access. Both of these factors influence the availability and costs of security measure. Weather patterns will influence the volume of visitors and the times they visit a site.

Prevailing climate conditions will affect both selection and operation of security hardware. Some sites are extraordinarily fragile. The structure itself may not be able to withstand the rigors of installation of security hardware. Some sites are damaged by the constant use by crowds of people. Accessibility may need to be curtailed or eliminated entirely in order to preserve the site itself. Changes in air, water and soil quality, resulting from this modern on a site. Security recommendations must pay heed to local customs, yet fulfill the directive of preservation and protection. Physical Security Analysis Will Measure Present-day Risks Once a site has been classified as historical, cultural or archaeological and the underlying influences at that site assessed, a physical security analysis must be conducted to discover the extent to which prior crimes and other incidents contribute to the risks at a site. Scrutiny of crimes and other incident is familiar ground to security specialist who uses this information to assess risks and make recommendations for measures to counteract those risks. A physical security analysis is defined as; an on-site analysis and documentation of a location to determine the foresee ability of crime and the adequacy of the existing physical security in order to establish a factual basis from which to make recommendations to reduce or remove the tangible opportunity for crime. Analyses are needed when:

(a) A site is opened to the public or archaeological work commences;
(b) A site is reactivated (changes may have taken place and new risk features may have been introduced;
(c) When a site has undergone a substantial change (such as a building expansion program, reduction in size, personnel changes, etc.)
(d) There is no record of a previous analysis;
(f) There is an unusual amount of loss taking place;
(g) There are changes in external conditions demongraphical considerations, political changes, and the like) h) there is a change in which security company is responsible for the protection of that site.

Security must select only those measures appropriate to a site. Appropriateness of a measure can only be determined after research into inherent pressures, underlying influences and present risks is completed. This research provides a totality of circumstances–the complex set of pressures and influences, many of which have their roots in the remote past. Security Measures Security has four general categories of measures. These measures can be used in various combinations and degrees in order to fulfill the purpose of security–the protection of lives and property. Security has at its disposal the use of impediments. Impediments accomplish what their name implies. These physical measures slowly down access to the person or thing deemed valuable. Examples of impediments include fences, walls, gates, and locking devices. The design, configuration, strength, manner of installation and use determine how quickly or slowly, easily or difficult, the access is. Detectors are another security measure. Detectors are another security measure. Detectors are most commonly associated with "burglar alarms" or "robbery alarms"–a mechanical, electrical, or electronic device that announces the presence of an intruder. These sensors are tools used to extend the range of human senses. People can and do use sight, sound, smell, taste and touch to perceive the environment around them and respond to their sensory perceptions.

The cost-effective generation and generation and delivery of electricity; the iniquitousness of telephone lines and wireless (via radio tower or satellite) communications have extended our sensory range. Tools to augment and supplement our sensory perceptions are not new. An early example of a burglar alarm is a floor in a 16th century C.E. Japanese temple. The floor was intently constructed to creak when a person walked on it. The armies of the Roman Empire posted geese as sentries. The third category of security measures is responders.

There must be a response to conditions in order to change those conditions. Security officers, police, a co-worker, a neighbour, a stranger, a lonely night watchman at a remote archaeological dig–each can be a responder. No one, whatever their function, can respond to conditions until they are made aware of those conditions. Notification comes through our personal sensory perceptions and is transmitted via detectors. The last category is neutrals. Neutral measures do not give advantage or disadvantage to any particular group. Neutrals are capable of benefitting all persons equally. The sun shines on every one. Artificial lighting which helps security personnel to see also provides illumination for vandals and thieves. The technology which security personnel use to talk with one another or to send and receive data is equally available to persons with less benign intentions.

Selection of Security Measures Selection of the proper security measures is based on asking certain question regarding the findings revealed by site research and analysis. Each measure has limitations. Security measures are selected based on their ability to remove, reduce or react (respond) to a set of (pre) determined risks where those risks are identified via an analysis of the totality of circumstances at a site. Proper selection of a set of security measures is based on an understanding of what those measures can and cannot accomplish as interpreted against a backdrop of the prevailing influences and pressures at a site. This understanding will help in finding the answers to the following questions. What criteria should be used for selecting a particular security measure?

Security measures, whatever their complexity or dependence on technology, are action taken as a method for achieving the stated goal of protection and preservation of a location and its structures. If a security measure can assist in this, then it may be appropriate for use. The measure must match the risk. Particular attention must be paid to the question: Will the security measure cause harm to the site? Is the security measure dependent upon technology that is either not available or unreliable at that location? Installing a fire suppression system which uses water may not be appropriate in locations without a dependable water supply or where water or other suppression agents (such as foam) will cause damage. How does the measure interact with the identified influences at a site? Impediments control access and thus are of assistance for traffic and other problems from crowds of people. The geographic location of a site may be enough of an access control measure to eliminate the need for fencing, gates, etc. It may not be feasible or aesthetically appropriate to install locking devices on certain structures. Religious practices, local customs and site fragility may require measures other than locking devices. Will it impede work at the site? This is particularly important at archaeological sites. Fencing may hinder access to and from excavations. Detection devices may cause electromagnetic interference with the advanced technology now used at many archaeological digs. Will the measure interfere with religious activities? Certain religions may restrict or bar altogether security personnel of a faith different from that celebrated at a location. It is possible that uniform styles and equipment will be dictated by religious principles. Will the use of the measure detract from the site's value? The preservation (in original or 'found' condition whenever possible) is of primary concern to those who administer these sites. Interference with the 'original state' for reasons of security may not be acceptable to curators, scholar, archaeologists or those who worship at a site. If the measure will physically alter the site itself, will this alteration be desirable or undesirable? The question hidden within this is, desirable by whom? Whatever measure is selected, that measure must contribute to the safety and protection of that site and not be implemented merely for the convenience of security practitioners or site administrators who wish "the latest thing". Will the measure increase the level of safety and amount of protection at a site?

Impediments which prevent access to dangerous areas such as deep wells will increase safety. A balance must be found between installing security measures which do increase safety and installing measures merely to impress a client or only for the convenience of the security company. What measures can be installed with a minimum amount of encroachment on that site? Security professional must carefully examine each recommendation and ask themselves if that measure intrudes unnecessarily into the activities which take place. Sometimes, security does not need to be visible or obvious in order to be effective. Can security react to an influence (e.g. environmental conditions such as weather or pollution) in order to reduce the amount of harm resulting from that influence? Harm can be reduced in a number of ways. Tents and other temporary covering can be erected over archaeological sites; fragile items can be relocated to museums; access control measures can be implemented to control expected crowds. Is this projected increase sufficient for present and projected conditions at that site? Many incidents are not predictable. Michelangelo's Pieta, on display at the Vatican in Rome, was attacked by a vandal several years ago. The marble sculpture was badly damaged. Since that time, impact-resistant glazing material, many inches thick, was installed in front of his work. In essence, this art was sealed off. This practice may not be feasible at other sites. Some locations cannot be 'sealed'. Religious practices may require that a location or object be fully accessible and in plain, unobstructed view. Many of the influences at a site cannot be changed. There is nothing that can be done about geography or weather patterns. Security cannot change local customs. An analysis of prior crimes and incidents yield trends and patterns, but it does not predict where or when. In these and other instances, security can only respond to existing conditions. Security practitioners can however analyze the probable events that many arise out of a set of existing conditions and develop planned responses. There are no easy answers to many of the questions posed in this paper. It is hoped that the asking of these questions will alert he reader to the problems that may not be immediately apparent when considering adding sites of this nature to your business. Each site experiences an evolution in its use. Security must be prepared to transform itself to meet each succeeding change.

Self Development

Renu Mattoo

Develop yourself before you think of developing others. With all the discussion on developing subordinates, we tend to forget that before we can think of their progress, we must take a look at ourselves, and locate areas in our own personality and skills that need attention. In fact, if a manager does not want to, or is not interested to enhance his own skills, he cannot develop those of his subordinates. If you do not feel committed to personal growth, an dare less than enthusiastic about your development, you will lose the zest of living, and the joy of achieving.

In the e-era, continuous and fast learning is critical: Continuous self-development has always been a valid requirement. Today, however, this development must come faster than ever, because we live in an era of quick an ever-increasing information and change. With new knowledge coming our wayt at break-neck from myriad media, learning is never complete, nor updated. You take a nap, and wake up to find your ernvironment has changed beyond recognitional! So, speed of self-development is critical. Fast self –development requires efficient and effective strategies.

Many people believe that development is a natural process, and that no special effort need be made for self-advancement. They may be right, but not quite, because the road to self-betterment has many barriers, most of them erected by the traveller himself. Some of these self imposed impediments are disinterest, laziness, the arrogance of I know-it-all", and the discomfort of change etc. These barriers are best tackled by a willingness to change, by welcoming and anticipating change, and seeking opportunities for self enrichment.

The first step to self-development is self-appraisal. You need to take a good, objective and intimate look at yourself. An ordered, effective way of doing that is by using the SWOT method. Identify first only your strengths. These are the knowledge, skills, positive behaviours, and attitudes you posses. Do not be modest. Write these down on paper. Look at this paper every day, and keep adding as you discover more strengths. As you note them doewn, you will be pleasantly surprised to see that you are good at many things. As your list increases in length, your self-confidence will get a boost. Your strengths are asset that you can use currently and in future to take decisions and to solve problems. After a week of listing only your strengths, now also and simultaneously, start to note your weaknesses, those areas that you are not strong in. This list will include all the knowledge and skills that you should have to be the best in your job, but either do not have at all or not enough. The list should also contain your behavioural weaknesses, and negative attitudinal traits.

While both strengths and weaknesses are internal to you, we turn to the external environment to identify opportunities and threats. Opportunities are all those favourable realities and situations around you that you can use for your advancement. The keener your eye to locate opportunities and the more developed your strengths, the greater the possibility of using opportunities for self-enrichment. Make a list of all opportunities in your immediate, middle distance and remote environment. Use the time dimension to see into the future for favourable situations. Given the shrinkage of both time and space, even the remote and far future are not really so. They will be within touching distance even as you think about them.

Now, consider the threats ion your environment. These are also realities, but those that could stall your attempts at growth and development. While some threats are patently clear, others lurk in the shadows. You need night vision-deep insight, and anticipation of what trends could create which negative state-to identify and locate these.

Now, what do you do with these four lists? You enhance and use your strengths; find ways to overcome your weaknesses; do not let opportunities slip by, but stay alert to them, and use as many as you can to advance yourself; and you use your strengths to reduce the severity of threats. Excellence, in other words, is an option, a choice for you.

To achieve excellence

1. Listen and Learn

Learn by reading, watching educative TV programmes, discussing with experts, and mainly by listening. Seek knowledge and develop new abilities, not only in your particular area of specialisation, but also in related areas.

2. Question and Clarify

Ask others to tell you what you are good at, and where you lack, invite thoughts on what you should be doing, how you can do better.

3. Risk Ridicule and Failure

Learn to take the risks of ridicule and even the failure of efforts as you try to develop your skills and knowledge. Do also know that there are three types of risks: One: Those not taken at all. Two: Reckless and rash ones. Three: Calculated risks. Take the last.

4. Plan and Practice

Make your own plans for advancement in your career. Do not wait for others to do that for you. No one can be as interested in your growth as you yourself. Practice your learning. There is no better way to develop any skill.

5. Develop a Winning Attitude

(a) Learn to love your job, and be enthusiastic about your responsibilities

(b) Use your strengths to shape your destiny by determining your environment.

Eight percent of employees like only twenty percent aspects of their job. This means that most people dislike major aspects of their job tasks. To be successful, however, it is essential that you like what you do, that you not only enjoy your work, but also value it greatly. Many people, however, believe that liking or disliking a job has a lost to do with the job itself, the kind of people one works with, the environment one works in, the chances of promotion and growth, etc. Success, they say, is dependent on extraneous factors.

The truth, however, is that we all have more power, greater energies, and more strength than we realise. Only the weak believe that circumstances control their destiny. The strong create their own environment. They are in control of circumstances, and take full responsibility for their situation.

You have the power to manage your environment, and take from it all that you need. If you do not do so, you will be left out in the cold. If you depend on others to help you, you may have to wait forever, for no one else – neither family, friends, bosses, nor colleagues – have the time, inclination, and skills to help you achieve success. Ultimately, it is what you do, and with what attitude you do it, that matters. So, how do you ensure your success? Here are some ways for you to consider.

6. Ensuring Sucess on the Job

- Move away from negative though patterns:

  [a] Why should I work any smarter, or harder, when there are no complaints about my performance? My boss and others are quite okay with my current output.

  [b] I want to acquire more skills, and perform better, but what can I do? My boss does not nominate me to any training pro-

grammes. He piles me with so much work that I have no time even to read the newspaper.

[c] I have no choice but to work harder, better, as that will please my boss and he will take care of me when the time comes for announcing increments, promotions and perks.

- Take personnel control of your life as you steer yourself towards your goal of self-development. A man reinvests in his own business not because someone tells him to do so, but because he wants to you will not be driven by an externally controlled motivation, but by an inner-determined inspiration. Your script will now read; I am going to develop myself because / want to, and I am capable of doing it. You are no more the couch that the railway engine pulls and pushes on the track to get moving. You are the engine, driven by an inner energy !! You have the choice.
- Decide what you want to do and how. Along with a change in attitude, you will need to first decide your job goals, and then develop a concrete, well-ordered, not haphazard, plan of action. It must sure what steps you will take, by when, and how. This plan must then be executed in a determined and proper manner.
- First, Picture your ideal job: Describe your fantasy: What would you rather be doing with what type of boss, colleagues, subordinates, in what kind of physical work environment. This is the profile of your current dream and goal. Once you know what you want to achieve, you can map the route to the destination. Write down in as much details as possible the various aspects of this dream job.
- Break the big picture into little snapshots. To develop a route, you need to identify landmarks on the way. You need to find places you can stop at, rest a while, refresh yourself, and then move on. These little images within the big picture are the various aspects of your dream job. They are the stepping stones, the rungs on the ladder to achieving the dream, and later, will help you move from one position to the next.
- Next, compare your dream job with what you currently have.

You are Assistant Manager in Administration, but want to be Head of Public Relations. You have a wimpy, weak Boss, but want a decisive, powerful one. You have a comer desk in a room full or noisy typists and typewriters, but you want a comer room with a word processor.

- Take charge. Be self-driven. Ask yourself what it is that YOU (not others) can do in order to change the picture. Note the alternatives open and available to you. Those that appears 'un-achievable' are so only because YOU believe they are impossible. Consider, for example, the first step in the direction of your goal. Ask "Cant I ask for a much lower position in PR? But, first, for them even to think of me as a possible candidate, I must acquire a relevant qualification."
- Treat your company as a client, and yourself as a supplier or contractor. This means looking after your company as you would look after your own business if you had one, and looking after your own interest, if you were a supplier. You would meet the demands of your client (your company to his satisfaction, and reinvest in various aspects of your business (your self) for further and further growth. This is the best way to ensure that you will be regular in following your plant.
- Take steps to improve your work atmosphere, by interacting with people around you in a more friendly, responsible, and positive way. Stop constantly complaining about your job, your boss, and your colleagues, Change your attitude. This is an essential step to enhancing your personal situation at work. Learn to smile, greet, make small talk, and offer to help others. Even if you have not got along very well with others in the past, as you initiate these friendly moves, many positive outcomes will emerge. Most importantly, your seniors will begin to have a better opinion of your abilities to work well with people. Though this will surprise some, the sincerity of your approach will soon be clear. People will soon recognise your changed attitude, and they will relate to you themselves in a positive, friendly manner. As you feel the warmth

of friendship, you will find your environment less stressful.

- Work towards getting the support of your seniors. Identify what your particular boss considers valuable traits. Does he like people to be casual and friendly, or serious and task – oriented? Should they be creative or logical an detail – oriented? Does he like 'yes' men, or those who can take an independent, but right stand? Since success depends in fair measures on support from the top, check which traits you need to develop in order to get this support. You do not have to be a sycophant that is the role of the weak and the inefficient. You do have to find ways to gain his support and respect, by becoming likeable, useful, and an effective achiever.
- Find ways to become more visible- pleasantly. Exhibit yourself positively. Write articles for trade journals, the house magazine, an for internal circulation. Involve yourself in company and local club activities, and become a member of professional bodies. Don't only become a member be an active one.
- Find yourself a mentor. Seek preferably someone a few rungs higher than you, power full, and himself well positioned. Seek his advice on what is the best way to position yourself in your kind of industry. Don't flaunt your closeness to him. In fact, I don't get too close to him, but admire an respect him from within touching distance.
- Promote yourself: Now, look for occasions to tell those who matter – your boss and other influential people in the company that you have the ability to contribute a lot more and that you want to be make yourself more valuable to the company. Though the performance review meeting is a good formal occasion, you do not have to wait for it to initiate dialogue with your boss. Pick a moment when your relationship with him is at its strongest, and say:" I am happy here, and with what I am doing. I want to make myself more valuable to the company. I believe i can do a lot more. What would you like me to do so that the value of my contribution increases?" Sometimes asking directly for a

promotion works, but not many situations allow for a direct: "I think I am ready for a promotion". Ask instead for what you can do to accomplish more, and achieve higher output.

- Develop your job skills: Seek actively to join training programme, and attend seminars. Let your boss know that you are interested in enhancing your skills, and that the benefits of such enrichment will go not only to you personally, but also the company. Apart from leading to your goals, this shows your motivation level.
- Offer new, constructive ideas to improve the performance of the whole department: If you are very good only in discharging your current, limited responsibilities, you may become so indispensable that your boss will never think of taking you away to another position. Even as you continue to perform well in your specified duties, let your boss know that you have lot more potential by offering constructive suggestions about improving your own output and that of the department. Develop new ideas. Think thee out well, so that they have unambiguous merit, and are clearly worth trying out. Taking the initiatives in this respect is a good way of presenting evidence of how well you could perform in other areas.
- Seek opportunities to help and support your boss and colleagues. The best way of demonstrating your worth an positive-ness is by volunteering to help others, including your boss. Look for opportunities – when your boss is working late or when a colleagues is struck with a stubborn problem. Not only does this foster better relations, it shows initiatives. Offer to add more to your tasks. It gives your boss a change to test your additional abilities,. Your offer may not always be taken up, you may see the opportunity but not have the time, but do not give up. Continue to look around for the next opportunity.
- Maintain a task and achievement dairy" Get into the habit of entering in a diary your daily/weekly tasks to be completed. In particular, enter in it (in different ink or in capital letters) any special achievements. This will help you keep track of your ac-

complishments. Let your boss see you use this diary. Also, when your boss gives you special instructions, note them down quickly in his presence. When you go to tell him that you have completed the task, again in his presence, refer to the diary. This tells him that you are maintaining a record of your achievements. One beneficial fallout of this habit is that a boss who habitually denies or alters instructions whimsically, or insists. I told you yesterday' when he did not, is more careful when dealing with you. Sometimes a boss may dispute the value of your achievements. The diary will provide hard evidence. A few days in advance of the annual performance review, find ways to let him know what you have accomplished.

- Look confident: Dress today ass if you were already tomorrow's position. Smile pleasantly, but not too widely. Stand and site straight. Walk briskly. Look people in the eye, but do not stare or glare at them. Speak clearly, and strongly. Know your facts. Plan and organise your life, stay focussed.

All of the above appears a tall order. But as you take one step at a time, the goal will get gradually closer to realisation. There is no reason why you cannot do what you want to. You have unique strengths and opportunities waiting to be used. Just do it!

About IISSM

The International Institute of Security and Safety Management (IISSM) is a non-profit educational society registered under the Indian Societies Act. It is devoted to promoting professionalism among security and loss prevention practitioners and creating all-round security awareness and consciousness amongst personnel in the related management cadre. IISSM is the Asia's oldest society in the field of security and loss prevention, which is continuously engaged for the last 21 years in disseminating latest developments and techniques in the area of security and loss prevention. It offers consultancy services and runs customised and thematic courses covering all aspects of industrial security, safety, fire prevention, loss prevention and allied subjects. It acts as a catalyst to bring professionals together for experience-sharing and updating professional knowledge through numerous training courses, seminars and workshops. It has an elaborate Professional Certification Programme for consultants, security and safety practitioners and bestows fellowship on highly deserving professionals.

Every year since 1991, IISSM has been organising international seminars, at times accompanied by exhibitions, attracting a large number of security and loss prevention professionals from India and abroad. Faculties in these seminars comprise well-known experts drawn from all over the world. Participants come from private sector industries, public sector undertakings, private security agencies, systems integrators, security equipment manufacturers, academic institutions, financial institutions, banking industry and the government departments. Countries so far represented in IISSM training programmes include Australia, Bangladesh, Belgium, Canada, Denmark, France, Germany, Hong Kong, Special Administrative Region, Indonesia, Israel, Kuwait, Malaysia, Mauritius, Mozambique, Nepal, Reunion Island, Saudi Arabia, Singapore, South Africa, Taiwan, Province of China, Thailand, Turkey, UK, USA, Zambia, Zimbabwe and India.

IISSM recently entered into an MoU with International Institute of Risk and Safety Management (IIRSM), UK, for accreditation of training centres, trainers and courses as also to run focused courses on Loss Prevention with IIRSM as a knowledge partner. A proposal to offer duel membership (IISSM & IIRSM) to each member is in advanced stages of consideration.

IISSM also proposes to conduct PG Diploma, Degree and MBA level courses (Level 1, 2 and 3) in collaboration with Indira Gandhi National Open University (IGNOU).

Suggested Readings

Norman Abrams *Anti-Terrorism and Criminal Enforcement*; Third Edition, 2009 (American Casebook Series) West Law School(12 August 2009)

Victor V Ramraj, Michael Hor, Kent Roach, George Williams Global *Anti-Terrorism Law and Policy;* Second Edition Cambridge University Press (31 January 2012)

Sandra Rollings-Magnusson *Anti-Terrorism: Security and Insecurity After 9/11;* Fernwood Publishing Co. Ltd. (1 September 2009)

Marcus Mann *Anti-Terrorism Risk Assessments: Effective Profiles, Predictions & Prevention;* Pearson Publications Company (January 2005)

Lorrie Faith Cranor, Simson Garfinkel *Security and Usability: Designing Secure Systems That People Can Use;* O'Reilly Media (September 1, 2005)

Thomas L Norman *Integrated Security Systems Design: Concepts, Specifications, and Implementation;* Butterworth-Heinemann (February 6, 2007)

Mary Lynn Garcia *The Design and Evaluation of Physical Protection Systems;* Butterworth-Heinemann (17 May 2001)

Mary Lynn Garcia *Design and Evaluation of Physical Protection Systems,*

Second Edition, Butterworth-Heinemann (10 October 2007)

Lawrence Fennelly *Effective Physical Security;* Third Edition Butterworth-Heinemann (22 December 2003)

The American Institute of Architects , Joseph A Demkin *Security Planning and Design: A Guide for Architects and Building Design Professionals;* Wiley (3 November 2003)

Steven P Lab *Crime Prevention;* Seventh Edition: *Approaches, Practices and Evaluations;* Anderson (15 April 2010)

Lawrence Fennelly *Handbook of Loss Prevention and Crime Prevention*; Fourth Edition, Butterworth-Heinemann (26 November 2003)

Deborah Mitchell Robinson *Policing and Crime Prevention* Prentice Hall (1 January 2002)

Dennis P Rosenbaum, Arthur J Lurigio, Robert C Davis *The Prevention of Crime: Social and Situational Strategies* (Contemporary Issues in Crime and Justice Series); Wadsworth Publishing; (9 April 1998)

Timothy Crowe M S Criminology, NCPI *Crime Prevention through Environmental Design*; Second Edition, Butterworth-Heinemann (13 April 2000)

NCPI *Understanding Crime Prevention*; Second Edition, Butterworth-Heinemann (26 April 2001)

Ingrid MR Verbauwhede (Editor) *Secure Integrated Circuits and Systems;* Springer (10 March 2010)

Michael Khairallah *Physical Security Systems Handbook: The Design and Implementation of Electronic Security Systems;* Butterworth-Heinemann (21 November 2005)

Bill Phillips *The Complete Book of Home, Site and Office Security: Selecting, Installing and Troubleshooting Systems and Devices;* McGraw-Hill (26 July 2006)

Jimmie W Hinze *Construction Safety;* Prentice Hall (11 September 1996)

J Gregory Service *Security for Hotels and Motels; A Perspectives on Liabilities;* Charles C Thomas Pub Ltd (January 1986)

David A Gordon *How to ramp up parking lot security. (garage parking security of Merck and Co. Inc.): An article from: Security Management*

[HTML] [Digital]

Yang Zhe Fang Min *shopping malls, supermarkets, Security and Loss Prevention Management* (1991)

Adam Sutton, Adrian Cherney, Rob White *Crime Prevention: Principles, Perspectives and Practices Cambridge University Press;* First Edition (21 July 2008)

Nick Tilley *Crime Prevention (Criminal Justice Series) Willan*; (3 February 2009)

Steven P Lab *Crime Prevention, Approaches, Practices and Evaluations Anderson*; Seventh Edition (15 April 2010)

Ronald V Clarke, Nick Tilley *Situational Prevention of Organised Crimes (Crime Science Series) Willan;* (23 March 2010)

Charles P Nemeth *Private Security and the Investigative Process, Auerbach Publications;* Third Edition (9 February 2010)

Sam C Sarkesian, John Allen Williams, Stephen J Cimbala, *US National Security: Policymakers, Processes and Politics Lynne Rienner Pub*; Four Edition; (30 November 2007)

Joanna Wayne *Security Measures (Harlequin Intrigue) Harlequin;* (1 September 2005)

Robert Fischer Ph D, Edward Halibozek MBA, David Walters *Introduction to Security, Eighth Edition Butterworth-Heinemann*; Eight Edition (1 April 2008)

Leonard J Hopper, Martha J Droge *Security and Site Design: A Landscape Architectural Approach to Analysis,* Assessment and Design Implementation Wiley; Frist Edition (March 11, 2005)

Jay Adkisson, Chris Riser *Asset Protection : Concepts and Strategies for Protecting Your Wealth McGraw-Hill*; Frist Edition; (18 June 2004)

Jabob T Alvarez *Social Security: Background Issues and Proposals;* Nova Science Pub Inc (31 December 2010)

Brian Gouin *Security Design Consulting: The Business of Security System;* Design Butterworth-Heinemann (16 May 2007)

Alan Jay Lincoln *Crime in the Library: A Study of Patterns, Impact, and Security Rr Bowker Llc* (October 1984)

Douglas C Montgomery *Design and Analysis of Experiments John Wiley*

& Sons; Sixth Edition (December 17, 2004)

Russell D Howard, James J F Forest, Joanne Moore *Homeland Security and Terrorism: Readings and Interpretations (The Mcgraw-Hill Homeland Security Series) McGraw-Hill;* First edition (16 August 2005)

Abeer Baker, Anat Matar *Threat: Palestinian Political Prisoners in Israel Pluto Press;* (15 June 2011)

Elsa Lee *Homeland Security and Private Sector Business: Corporations' Role in Critical Infrastructure Protection;* Auerbach Publications (22 October 2008)

Charles P Pfleeger, Shari Lawrence Pfleeger *Analyzing Computer Security: A Threat / Vulnerability / Countermeasure Approach Prentice Hall;* First Edition (4 September 2011)

Peter Thermos, Ari Takanen Securing *VoIP Networks: Threats, Vulnerabilities, and Countermeasures Addison-Wesley Professional;* First Edition (11 August 2007)

Frederick S Calhoun, Steve W Weston J D *Threat Assessment and Management Strategies: Identifying the Howlers and Hunters CRC Press;* Fisrt Edition (6 October 2008)

Mani Bhushan Prasad *Reactions to Threat: a Study of Personality Patterns of Repressers and Sensitizers National Publishing House;* First Edition (1 January 1979)

David F Ferraiolo, D Richard Kuhn, Ramaswamy Chandramouli *Role-Based Access Control, Artech Print on Demand; Second Edition* (31 January 2007)

Messaoud Benantar *Access Control Systems: Security, Identity Management and Trust Models Springer; Softcover reprint of hardcover* First Edition (29 October 2010)

Anthony C Caputo *Digital Video Surveillance and Security Butterworth-Heinemann* (15 March 2010)

Fredrik Nilsson,Communications Axis *Intelligent Network Video: Understanding Modern Video Surveillance Systems CRC Press;* Har/Dvdr Edition (10 September 2008)

Bill Phillips *Master Locksmithing: An Expert's Guide to Master Keying, Intruder Alarms, Access Control Systems, High-Security Locks... McGraw-Hill*

Professional; First Edition (27 August 2007)

Dale L June *Introduction to Executive Protection: CRC Press;* Second Edition (17 January 2008)

Robert L Oatman *The Art of Executive Protection R.L. Oatman & Associates;* First Edition (June 1997)

Robert L Oatman *Tree Top Studio (Illustrator) Executive Protection New: Solutions for a New Era Noble House;* First Edition (13 June 2006)

A Hunsicker *Advanced Skills in Executive Protection;* Universal Publishers (20 March 2010)

Philip Holder, Donna Lea Hawley *The Executive Protection Professional's Manual Butterworth-Heinemann* (16 September 1997)

David S Katz, Ilan Caspi *Executive's Guide to Personal Security Wiley;* First Edition (6 June 2003)

Robert L Oatman *Executive Protection: Rising to the Challenge ASIS International;* First Edition (1 September 2009)

Jan Reber, Paul Shaw *Executive Protection Manual Mti Teleprograms;* Second Edition (June 1980)

John Shook *Managing to Learn: Using the A3 Management Process Lean Enterprises Inst Inc;* First Edition (June 2008)

Project Management Institute *A Guide to the Project Management Body of Knowledge, (PMBOK Guides) Project Management Institute;* Third Edition (January 2004)

G Edward Evans, Patricia Layzell Ward *Management Basics for Information Professionals, Neal Schuman Publishers;* Second Edition (1 August 2007)

Artie Mahal *How Work Gets Done: Business Process Management, Basics and Beyond;* First Edition, Technics Publications, LLC (10 October 2010)

Ros Jay *How to Manage Your Boss: Developing the Perfect Working Relationship Financial Times Management;* (June 2002)

Andy S Grove *One-on-One With Andy Grove: How to Manage Your Boss, Yourself, and your Coworkers Penguin Books;* (1988)

Kristie Kennard *How to Manage Your Boss: Build a Partnership with Your Boss That Will Make You Both Successful;* Elevanth Printing Edition,

National Press Publications (1 January 1996)

George E Berkley *How to Manage Your Boss Prentice Hall Trade* (May 1985)

Gavin de Becker *Fear Less: Real Truth About Risk, Safety, and Security in a Time of Terrorism Little, Brown and Company;* First Edition (4 January 2002)

William M Epps *Terrorism and Personal Security: Reduce Your Chances of Becoming a Target South-Western;* First Edition,Educational Publication (23 March 2005)

K C Poulin, Charles P Nemeth *Private Security and Public Safety: A Community-Based Approach Prentice Hall;* First Edition (19 July 2004)

Mary Lynn Garcia *Design and Evaluation of Physical Protection Systems, Butterworth-Heinemann;* Second Edition (10 October 2007)

Mary Lynn Garcia *Vulnerability Assessment of Physical Protection Systems Butterworth-Heinemann;* First Edition (21 November 2005)

David G Patterson *Implementing Physical Protection Systems: A Practical Guide ASIS International;* First Edition (January 2005)

Harold A Bennett *Design guidance and evaluation methodology for fixed-site physical protection systems University of Michigan Library;* (1 January 1980)

Michael Khairallah *Physical Security Systems Handbook: The Design and Implementation of Electronic Security Systems Butterworth-Heinemann* (21 November 2005)

Roger Geary *Policing Industrial Disputes: 1893 to 1985 Cambridge University Press;* First Edition (17 February 2011)

Quint C Thurman, Andrew Giacomazzi *Controversies in Policing (Controversies in Crime and Justice) Anderson;* First Edition (15 June 2005)

Laurence Alison, Jonathan Crego *Policing Critical Incidents: Leadership and Critical Incident Management Willan* (1 February 2008)

Peter Piazza *Hurdles to Cyberjustice.(Brief Article): An article from: Security Management [HTML] [Digital]*

Deborah E Bouchoux *Protecting Your Company's Intellectual Property: A Practical Guide to Trademarks, Copyrights, Patents & Trade Secrets AMACOM* (15 April 2001)

Melvyn Leffler *A Preponderance of Power: National Security, the Truman Administration, and the Cold War (Stanford Nuclear Age Series) Stanford University Press* (1 July 1993)

Walter Dean Myers *Ann Grifalconi (Illustrator) Patrol: An American Soldier in Vietnam HarperCollins* (4 January 2005)

Eric D Knapp *Industrial Network Security: Securing Critical Infrastructure Networks for Smart Grid, SCADA, and Other Industrial Control Systems Syngress;* First Edition (29 August 2011)

Charles A Sennewald CPP *Effective Security Management, Butterworth-Heinemann;* Fifth Edition (28 April 2011)

Department of Defense *National Industrial Security Program Operating Manual (NISPOM);* Red Bike Publishing (22 July 2010)

Hedieh Nasheri *Economic Espionage and Industrial Spying (Cambridge Studies in Criminology) Cambridge University Press* (6 December 2004)

Ronald L Mendell *The Quiet Threat: Fighting Industrial Espionage in America Charles C Thomas Pub Ltd;* Second Edition (December 2010)

Shepherd Mead *How to Succeed at Business Spying by Trying: A Novel About Industrial Espionage The Shepherd Mead Estate* (31 January 2011)

Kevin D Murray *Business Spies and the top 10 spy-busting tips they don't want you to know! (Personal Counterespionage Series) Spybusters, LLC;* First Edition (17 July 2010)

Eamon Javers Broker, Trader, Lawyer Spy *The Secret World of Corporate Espionage HarperBusiness;* First Edition (9 February 2010)

Gerard Honey *Electronic Access Control Newnes* (18 April 2000)

Michael Khairallah *Physical Security Systems Handbook: The Design and Implementation of Electronic Security Systems Butterworth-Heinemann* (21 November 2005)

Gursharan Varandani *Social security for industrial workers in India;* Deep & Deep Publications (1987)

Dipak Haldar *Industrial Security in India South Asia Books* (December 1986)

Ramgopal Agarwala (Editor), Nagesh Kumar (Editor), Michelle Riboud (Editor) Reforms *Labour Markets, and Social Security in India Oxford University Press, USA;* First Edition (11 March 2004)

Bal Krishan *Industrial securities market in India;* Commonwealth Publishers (1989)

Anne Bruce, James S Pepitone *Motivating Employees McGraw-Hill;* First Edition (1 October 1998)

Carlos A Conejo *Motivating Hispanic Employees: A Practical Guide to Understanding and Managing Hispanic Employees Multicultural Press;* Second Edition (July 2001)

Allen Amason *Strategic Management: From Theory to Practice Routledge;* First Edition (9 December 2010)

Darlene Van Tiem, James L Moseley, Joan C Dessinger *Fundamentals of Performance Technology, International Society for Performance Improvement;* Second Edition (April 2004)

John Adair *Effective Motivation: How to Get Extraordinary Results from Everyone (Effective Series) Macmillan UK* (1 May 2002)

William F Baker, Michael O'Malley PhD *Leading with Kindness: How Good People Consistently Get Superior Results AMACOM* (13 August 2008)

Morten Hansen *Collaboration: How Leaders Avoid the Traps, Create Unity, and Reap Big Results Harvard Business School Press* (11 May 2009)

Jack Wiley, Brenda Kowske *Respect: Delivering Results by Giving Employees What They Really Want Pfeiffer;* First Edition (18 October 2011)

Lee Colan *Engaging the Hearts and Minds of All Your Employees: How to Ignite Passionate Performance for Better Business Results McGraw-Hill;* First Edition (15 August 2008)

Aleks Srbinoski *Motivation Now: Productivity and Persuasion Secrets For Modern Day Excellence and Effectiveness (Success Secrets Series) Fulfilling Happiness;* First Edition (26 August 2011)

Herbert L Petri, John M Govern *Motivation: Theory, Research, and Applications (with InfoTrac);* Fifth Edition, Wadsworth Publishing (8 August 2003)

Johnmarshall Reeve *Understanding Motivation and Emotion Wiley;* Fifth Edition (24 November 2008)

Edward L Deci, Richard Flaste *Why We Do What We Do: Understanding Self-Motivation Penguin (Non-Classics);* (1 August 1996)

Michael Klare, Yogesh Chandrani *World Security: Challenges for a New Century;* Third Edition, Wadsworth Publishing (15 December 1997)

Gal Luft, Anne Korin *Energy Security Challenges for the 21st Century: A Reference Handbook (Contemporary Military, Strategic, and Security Issues) Praeger* (10 August 2009)

Colin S Gray *National Security Dilemmas: Challenges and Opportunities Potomac Books Inc.* (31 January 2009)

Michael E. Brown *Grave New World: Security Challenges in the 21st Century Georgetown University Press* (29 July 2003)

Mark Egan, Tim Mather *The Executive Guide to Information Security: Threats, Challenges, and Solutions Addison-Wesley Professional;* First Edition (10 December 2004)

Avery Goldstein *Rising to the Challenge: China's Grand Strategy and International Security (Studies in Asian Security) Stanford University Press;* First Edition (13 April 2005)

Ryan Fries, Mashrur Chowdhury, Jeffrey Brummond *Transportation Infrastructure Security Utilizing Intelligent Transportation Systems Wiley;* (10 November 2008)

Agusti Solanas, Antoni MartA-nez-bal *Advances in Artificial Intelligence for Privacy Protection and Security (Intelligent Information Systems)* World Scientific Publishing Company (30 September 2009)

Sundaresan Jayaraman, Paul Kiekens, Ana Marija Grancaric *Intelligent Textiles for Personal Protection and Safety IOS Press* (30 April 2006)

Pedro U Lima, George N Saridis *Design of Intelligent Control Systems Based on Hierarchical Stochastic Automata (Series in Intelligent Control and Intelligent Automation)* World Scientific Pub Co Inc (June 1996)

Douglas E Campbell *The intelligent threat. (special section - Computer-Information Security: Getting the Protection You Need): An article from: Security Management [HTML] [Digital]*

Jerry H Ratcliffe *Intelligence-led Policing Willan* (2 March 2008)

Jerry Ratcliffe *Strategic Thinking in Criminal Intelligence Federation Pr;* Second Edition (June 2009)

A Hunsicker *The Fine Art of Executive Protection: Handbook for the Executive Protection Officer* Universal Publishers (28 December 2007)

Ronald Kessler *In the President's Secret Service: Behind the Scenes with Agents in the Line of Fire and the Presidents They Protect Broadway;* Reprint Edition (3 August 2010)

Louis William Rogers *Self Development and the Way to Power Nabu Press* (22 February 2010)

David B Peterson, Mary Dee Hicks *Development First: Strategies for Self-Development Personnel Decisions Intl;* First Edition (June 1995)

Steve Pavlina *Personal Development for Smart People: The Conscious Pursuit of Personal Growth Hay House* (15 October 2009)

Karl Moore *The Secret Art of Self-Development: 16 little-known rules for eternal happiness & freedom [Kindle Edition]*

Joseph J Luciani *The Power of Self-Coaching: The Five Essential Steps to Creating the Life You Want Wiley;* First Edition (4 August 2004)

Gene Tucker, James F Broder *Risk Analysis and the Security Survey, Butterworth-Heinemann;* Third Edition (8 March 2006)

James L Schaub, Ken D Biery CPP *The Ultimate Security Survey, Second Edition Butterworth-Heinemann;* Second Edition (11 September 1998)

James F Broder, Gene Tucker *Risk Analysis and the Security Survey, Butterworth-Heinemann;* Fourth Edition (20 January 2012)

Small Arms Survey Geneva *Small Arms Survey 2011: States of Security Cambridge University Press;* First Edition (15 August 2011)

James L Schaub, Toni Ames *Ultimate Telecommunications Security Survey Butterworth-Heinemann* (7 July 1995)